Clients Forever

CLIENTS FOREVER

HOW YOUR CLIENTS CAN BUILD YOUR BUSINESS FOR YOU

Doug Carter

Jenni Green

McGraw-Hill

New York   Chicago   San Francisco   Lisbon   London
Madrid   Mexico City   Milan   New Delhi   San Juan
Seoul   Singapore   Sydney   Toronto

The *McGraw·Hill* Companies

2 3 4 5 6 7 8 9 0   AGM/AGM   0 9 8 7 6 5 4

ISBN 0-07-140256-X

McGraw-Hill books are available at special quantity discounts to use as premiums and sales promotions, or for use in corporate training programs. For more information, please write to the Director of Special Sales, Professional Publishing, McGraw-Hill, Two Penn Plaza, New York, NY 10121-2298. Or contact your local bookstore.

 This book is printed on recycled, acid-free paper containing a minimum of 50% recycled, de-inked fiber.

Library of Congress Cataloging-in-Publication Data

Carter, Doug.
    Clients forever : how your clients can build your business for
you / by Doug Carter and Jennifer Green.
        p. cm.
    Includes index.
    ISBN 0-07-140256-X (alk. paper)
    1. Selling. 2. Customer relations. I. Green, Jennifer. II.
Title.
    HF5438.25.C367 2003
    658.85—dc21

2002153055

CONTENTS

CHAPTER 1

WHAT IF ALL YOUR CLIENTS LOVED YOU?

People often get uncomfortable when *clients* and *love* show up in the same sentence. One word belongs in the glossary of *Business for Beginners*; the other comes from Touchy-Feely 101.

When most people meet an idea that makes them squirm, they unconsciously find ways to get more comfortable. For instance, you might mentally plug *what* and *do* into the title of this chapter. You'd then read it like this: What if all your clients loved what you do? It's easy to imagine *doing* something your clients would love.

Here's another mental trick you might use if the title of this chapter rubs you the wrong way. Did you delete *all*? The chapter title would then become "What If Some Unspecified Number of Your Clients Loved You?" What if, say, ten of your clients bonded with you enough to write you into their wills? What if five thought you were the bee's knees?

All joking aside, these might be good questions to ponder. We'd even wager that your business life would improve if you gave them some thought.

But they're not the radical, life-changing question we're posing. Take a deep breath.

Consider what life would be like if *all* your clients loved *you*. How would you feel—and how would your business be different—if the prospect of an appointment with you made your clients smile? What if they screened all their calls, answering only those from their significant others, their children, and *you*? What if they couldn't wait to tell all their friends and relatives about you?

Imagine, too, that you loved your clients in return. Not that you'd hug and gaze into each other's eyes when you were together. Nor would you break into the first bars of "Kumbaya." But what if your business relationships were an integral part of what made—and kept—life rich and meaningful for you? Your clients would contribute to your economic success, sure, but their importance to you would extend far beyond their financial value.

YOUR EXTRAORDINARY CLIENT

The idea of all your clients loving you may seem a little far-fetched to you right now. However, you probably already have one or more client relationships that come very close to what we're talking about.

Most salespeople can identify at least one client who seems extraordinary. Our workshop participants describe theirs in terms like these:

He's completely satisfied with what we've done for him; he keeps coming back. It's more than that, though. We hang out together, too.

Wherever I've gone, this one guy has come with me.

I've had one particular client for eight years; he's bought a product from me six or seven times. Every time we talk, he tells me how good I am. He thanks me very much for everything I've done, for taking care of him and his family. He keeps giving me referrals. If I want to feel good about myself on a given day, I'll call him.

Odds are, you have a similar client relationship. The two of you may even feel as close as family members. If you want to go out for lunch, you might invite this individual along simply because you enjoy his or her company. If you desperately needed to make a sale—let's say you were in a contest—you could consider calling this client. "Hey," you might imagine saying, "I really need you to spring for something. Will you help me out?"

You know he probably would—and that's precisely why you'll never ask. You also reckon that, even if you never sell another thing, the two of you will stay in touch.

From your perspective, this client is truly extraordinary. He or she stands alone, in a completely different category than the rest of the perfectly nice but ordinary mortals who make up your book.

Nobody ever told you that you'd have a client who felt so much like a friend. The boundary between *business* and *pleasure*, the one that's supposed to keep them from mixing, is stretched so thin it barely exists. Maybe you feel almost guilty taking more money from this person. Surely, you think, he or she is only buying from me because of our bond.

Exactly.

Maybe that's not the *only* reason your extraordinary client keeps doing business with you, but it's one of the best. He or she could likely get the same product and the same service anywhere else. It's the relationship that keeps this buyer coming back to you.

Maybe, after all this, you're still uncomfortable with the notion that your extraordinary client loves you. Here's what we mean by *love*; you can substitute whatever words you want—just don't change the meaning. Your extraordinary client feels deep affection for you. He or she respects and cares about you. Your extraordinary client delights in your success and happiness and highly values your opinion.

Love is just our shorthand.

FROM ONE TO MANY

Now that you know what we mean by extraordinary clients and how it applies to your current book of business, consider this:

Extraordinary clients can be ordinary.

That's right. The kind of client you've previously thought of as an exception can make up the majority of your book. Your business life can be full of clients who love you—and whom you love.

Will every client relationship reach this pinnacle and stay there 100 percent of the time? Probably not. If you've ever had a long-term bond with a friend or a spouse, you know that connections develop and deepen over time. Relationships have a natural ebb and flow. They can even have finite lifespans.

So even when your business life becomes much more emotionally and financially rewarding, you'll probably still have a few challenging—or merely ordinary—clients. However, they'll represent a smaller proportion of your total business activity.

So, let's go back to the original question. What if all your clients loved you?

It would be very, very good for your business.

Just ask Steven McGuffey and Bill Fernandez of Mountain West Asset Management Company in Palo Alto, California. Before transforming their business, McGuffey and Fernandez employed six staff members to help service 831 clients. They spent an average of sixty-two hours a week managing $74 million in assets.

One of their first transformational steps was to sell off $15 million worth of assets under management—the portfolios of nearly 600 clients with whom they shared ordinary relationships.

Within a year, McGuffey and Fernandez went from managing $59 million of assets to overseeing $102 million. Their reduced workload means they only need one full-time staff member. All three take Fridays off as part of a twenty-eight hour workweek. They often fail to get all twenty-eight hours in, too. McGuffey took 151 days off in 2000 while Fernandez skipped 139.

Are they suffering financially? Not at all. Profits are up 24 percent, and personal before-tax income is up 41 percent.

YEAH, BUT...

Of course, their results are outstanding because Fernandez looks like John Travolta, has a brogue like Sean Connery's, and counts the Dalai Lama as a close personal friend. McGuffey? He's a decorated war hero and the spitting image of Denzel Washington; he dedicates his spare time to helping elderly nuns teach underprivileged kids how to read. You couldn't possibly do as well as they've done.

Not.

McGuffey and Fernandez are two ordinary guys who decided to capitalize on the client relationships they enjoyed the most. They took a risk—they won't deny that selling a portion of their business was a little scary. It paid off handsomely, however.

It paid off in both financial and emotional terms. Their impressive income hike almost overshadows the *thirty-four-hour* shrinkage in their workweek. Sounds good, doesn't it? Who wouldn't prefer to work less than half as much and make 40 percent more money?

There's also a huge intangible payoff. Imagine putting in many fewer hours, making more money—and working almost exclusively with clients you truly enjoy, respect, and care for.

YEAH, BUT (PART 2) . . .

So far, we've apparently based the whole premise of *Clients Forever* on the experience of just two guys. They're great guys, but we bet you'd like more evidence anyway.

In 1995, an article entitled "Why Satisfied Customers Defect" appeared in the *Harvard Business Review*. Thomas O. Jones and W. Earl Sasser, Jr., service management experts and educators, revealed some astonishing research findings.

Across five industries, they measured customer satisfaction on a five-point scale (1 = completely dissatisfied, 2 = dissatisfied, 3 = neutral, 4 = satisfied, 5 = completely satisfied). Jones and Sasser then correlated these ratings with customer loyalty, which they measured by a customer's stated intention to repurchase and his or her actual repurchasing and referral behaviors.

Some of their findings held no surprise. You'd expect completely dissatisfied and dissatisfied customers to defect. You'd expect neutral customers to shop around. But, if you're like most service managers and providers, you'd lump together the customers who rated their experience with your company as a 4 or 5. You'd think satisfied and completely satisfied customers would have no reason to defect.

You would be making a mistake.

The rating that distinguishes customers who stick with a product or service from those who defect is 5, not 4. Put another way, completely satisfied customers are loyal; merely satisfied customers are not.

(Jones and Sasser's fascinating article contains a treasure trove of strategies for improving customer satisfaction ratings. We encourage you to read it, and you can download it in PDF format for a small fee at www.hbsp.harvard.edu.)

Jones and Sasser call completely satisfied customers and clients *loyalists* and *apostles*. They stick with you, and they spread the word. Some estimate that completely satisfied customers are 400 percent more likely to make multiple purchases and give unsolicited referrals to you than are customers who are merely satisfied.

Jones and Sasser's article concludes with a quotation from Horst Schulze, then president and COO of the Ritz-Carlton Hotel Company, winner of the 1992 Malcolm Baldrige National Quality Award:

> Unless you have 100% customer satisfaction—and I don't mean that they are just satisfied, I mean that they are excited about what you are doing—you have to improve.

Hmmm, complete customer satisfaction. Customers and clients who are excited about what you're doing.

Sounds a little like our definition of love.

YEAH, BUT (PART 3) . . .

Right about now, when an idea sounds as if it might be both fun and financially rewarding, some people step on the emotional and mental brakes. If you slam on the brakes in a car, you get a high-pitched squeal. If you apply your internal brakes, you get these sound effects:

Yeah, right.

Or this:

Sounds too easy.

Or this:

[Press your lips together lightly and blow. You just heard a cynical sputter.]

In the first part of our workshops, we talk about how every sales professional can have a book of business like the one we've described. Then we ask the cynics in the audience to raise their hands.

Some participants don't raise their hands until they find out why we want to know. Now *those* are cynics.

Cynicism and skepticism are universal human traits. There's nothing wrong with being cynical. In fact, cynics are generally sales professionals with lots of experience.

They have lots of experience with broken promises and unfulfilled commitments: *If you need anything, just give me a call. You'll have that tomorrow. The check's in the mail. I'll get back to you.*

And the perennial favorite: *I'll still love you in the morning.* Different topic, same lesson.

Cynics have learned, through trial and error, that caution is better than courage. They've learned that if you don't try anything new, you won't feel hurt or disappointed.

There's a popular misconception that cynics are insensitive people who don't care. That couldn't be more incorrect. Truly insensitive people are *so* insensitive that they don't realize they're insensitive. They keep plowing full steam ahead; it never occurs to them that they might end up hurt or disappointed or that they might hurt or disappoint someone else.

Cynics, on the other hand, are people who care so much that they've stopped giving their all. They test the waters before plunging in. They take on only the parts of a new process that feel safest, figuring they'll ease into the rest if the first bits go well. They look for what's wrong with something before they look for what's right.

So, are you feeling skeptical? Cautious?

Good. We're suggesting that some rather dramatic changes are possible. A little caution seems prudent.

But we'd like to strike a bargain with you. Since excess caution can also prevent you from experiencing these changes, we're going to ask you to check out your level of cynicism—and then decide whether to keep reading *Clients Forever*.

HOW CYNICAL ARE YOU?

Please follow the directions below without skipping ahead. We realize that sentence alone is enough to make some of you skip ahead to see what we're hiding, but resist the temptation. You'll get more out of this if you just trust us for a page or so.

Here we go:

Hold *Clients Forever* in your left hand. Turn your right hand palm up. Flex your fingers slightly and spread them gently apart.

Imagine that the basin formed by your right hand holds all the experiences you've had selling products and services to other people over the last four or ten or fifteen or twenty-seven years. Your whole career as a sales professional—up until this moment—rests in the palm of your right hand. Good and less-than-exciting clients, successful and failed sales, multiple employers and positions, prosperity, tight cash flow, satisfaction and stress—they all go in your right hand.

Close your eyes for a moment, if you want or need to do so. Make sure to get the imaginary sense that you're holding your past in your hand.

Now read to the end of the next paragraph, then do what it says. Avoid skipping ahead. Just trust us, for Pete's sake—you'll see why in a minute.

When you're ready, lift your right hand to your face, palm inward. Rest the heel of your hand gently against your nose. Leave it there while you observe what's directly in front of your eyes and how much of your vision beyond your hand is blocked. Then continue on to the next paragraph.

Your hand represents your past. We call it *the squid*. It's icky, it's sticky, and it can keep you from seeing where you could go. (You can have your right hand back, by the way.)

We asked you to use your hand so you could see the squid in three dimensions. If you're like most of us, the previous experiences that your hand represent obscured your view almost completely. You couldn't see what was directly in front of you because your past was in the way. You couldn't even read the words on this page without your past interfering.

If you're like most of us, the squid remains—even after you drop your hand. In fact, an invisible squid lives on your face; you just haven't been aware of it before. Every time you make an unconscious connection between the past and your future possibilities, you're seeing the squid.

The following are two examples. First, let's say you've been a sales professional for five years. During that time, you've attended a few sales seminars and tried some of the techniques you learned there. You've read the best-selling books and done the same thing. Every time, you've experienced, at best, a temporary blip up in your sales figures. Frankly, you haven't been all that comfortable with what you've learned in books and seminars either.

Now, how likely is it that you think *Clients Forever* or any other book or seminar could help you create permanent change? Not very. Your experience seems to show you that sales training is a less-than-terrific investment of time and money. You're not sure what the answer is, but you doubt that you'll find it here. Some people call that common sense; we call it the squid.

Let's look at another hypothetical example. Mary's been a financial advisor for seven years. Her first year was very quiet; sometimes, it seemed as if she was the only person who knew or cared she was in business.

In her second year, she made a series of sales to the Barkers, a middle-income married couple in their mid-forties with three children, one of whom was due to start college within four years. The Barkers, pleased with her personal attention, gave her the first bit of referred business that panned out.

The referral happened to be to Mr. Barker's best friend and his wife, the Browns. The Browns were the same age as the Barkers and had two kids, one of whom was due to start college within five years.

Mary quickly made a sale to the second couple, too. Unconsciously, she started looking for prospects who were middle-income married couples in their mid-forties with two or more children. She took on several as clients and started to earn a reasonable income.

Over time, because she was unconsciously drawn to and more confident with prospects who fit the demographic profile of the Barkers, she "learned" that her batting average was better with them. Clients of varying ages, income levels, and family constellations would have been an enjoyable—and more profitable—mix, but Mary believed her strengths as a salesperson fit a particular client profile.

In other words, she let her past experiences determine her future direction. As was true for Mary, how your business has evolved in the past—everything that's happened until now—influences what you believe is possible in the future. As far as you're concerned, the evidence is clear—and right in front of your face.

Later, you can explore your beliefs about your business and

how they affect what you think is possible from this point on. For now, ask yourself this question: What were you looking at a few moments ago? Were you staring at the palm of your right hand or into the belly of the squid?

IF IT WAS YOUR RIGHT HAND

If you doubt the existence of the squid—the compelling, constant influence that your past has on your present and future—you probably also doubt that reading *Clients Forever* could truly change your experience. It's fine with us if you stop reading at this point. What we're suggesting in these pages isn't a good fit for everyone, and we commend your candor and self-awareness.

Thank you very much for buying *Clients Forever*; we hope your copy finds a loving home with someone else.

HELP! THERE'S A SQUID ON MY FACE!

If you had a Jules Verne moment, keep reading.

As we were saying, skepticism is fine. There's nothing wrong with being a cynic other than its tendency to suck the very life out of you. You obviously want to live more than half a life.

Glad you're still with us.

Having declared your lack of cynicism—or at least that you're not adrift in a sea of cynicism—by reading on, you deserve a little fun. Think of it as squid relief.

Consider the possibility that your business could be made up almost exclusively of the type of clients you believe to be extraordinary. Read that sentence again. There's a reason it begins with the words *Consider the possibility*.

That's all you have to do at this point. We're not asking you to plunge right in, as earnest and chipper as an Up with People recruit.

No, we suspect you might prefer to sidle unseen into the

metaphorical back row. Go ahead. Just promise three things: You'll think about the possibility that all your clients could love you, you'll do the exercises, and you'll see if the idea of transforming your business takes on life.

FIRST, KNOW WHAT YOU WANT

So let's get started. No more sea creatures. Just you and the extraordinary clients you want more of.

One principle underlying *Clients Forever* is that the more clarity you have about what you really want, the more likely you are to experience it. For instance, the more specifically you understand your extraordinary clients, the more easily you can recognize other individuals with the same characteristics. While reading this book, you'll have several opportunities to crystallize in your mind exactly what you enjoy about these individuals and your relationships with them.

You probably already know about defining your desired client in terms of demographics: industry, income, age, gender, occupation, and so forth. Later, you'll have a chance to define— or redefine—your extraordinary client in these terms.

We'll start, though, with something more subtle—shared psychology. Your client's attitudes, beliefs, and ideals help create the sense of connection you feel. Let's separate that global sense of affinity into the elements that are most important to you.

If one of your clients fits our general description of an extraordinary one, bring that individual to mind. If the notion of an extraordinary client is completely new to you, think of a colleague or coworker relationship you enjoy. These ties can turn into personal friendships, though, so choose a newer relationship or try to recall the time before you felt comfortable discussing personal matters.

Create a short list of what you enjoy about working with

this person. Be sure to keep one individual in mind as you do so or you'll be tempted to generalize to what you think you *ought* to like. Distinguish, too, between what impresses you and what you like. Enumerate five to ten traits.

Think about things like how he communicates with you, her level of energy and enthusiasm, his priorities, her willingness to act, how receptive he is to your input—to name just a few. Here are some samples from actual lists to get you started.

Funny
Gets my jokes
Very intelligent
Articulate
Decisive
Passionate
Altruistic
Generous
Honorable
Pays right away
Helps me learn
Knows company needs to work with me
Doesn't quibble about my price
Fun and easy to work with
Cares about employees and themselves
Pays correctly and quickly
Highly vocal about the positive results of working with me
Keeps great records of the results of working with me
Proactively installs the skills and systems I teach

Avoid copying an item verbatim. If something resonates for you, take the time to restate it in your own words. Although you *are* taking a close look inside your extraordinary client's head, this exercise isn't brain surgery. It only requires a few moments of concentrated attention; use the space on the next page.

SECOND, KNOW WHY YOU WANT IT

Warning: Poetic reference just ahead. If poetry puts you off, be grateful for the change from the sea creatures theme.

In 1920, Robert Frost paid homage to choice in "The Road Not Taken." Many people recall the part about the road less traveled by and what a difference taking it made, but there's a juicy bit that comes a few lines earlier.

Standing at a fork in the road, a traveler considers taking one path and coming back later to try the other. However, he realizes that he won't return once he starts down either one. Whichever path he takes will lead him farther and farther away from the fork in the road.

Imagine now, for a moment, that you're standing at a fork, considering which way to take. The path to the left is a perfect continuation of the road you've traveled until now. It's a straight, tree-lined arrow to the horizon. No surprises lurk, no disasters or windfalls await you. Your companions along that road stand and sit quietly in the woods beside it—they're in no hurry to greet you. They're much like the clients you already have. Nice enough people, but when you take them to lunch, it will feel deductible.

Imagine yourself five years down this road. What's your daily experience like? Write three or four words below to describe it.

How's your income?

Your level of enthusiasm?

What happens after twenty years down that road?

Now shift your attention to the road on the right. Imagine that it's identical to the one on the left, with one exception. Your companions on this road are clones, so to speak, of your extraordinary client. These individuals share the characteristics you listed above in abundance. They can't wait for you to reach them; they're waving at you, energetic and impatient.

Imagine yourself five years down this road. What's your daily experience like? A few more words, please.

(By the way, this is between you and the book. Nobody will witness the heights to which you allow your imagination to soar.)

How's your income?

Your level of enthusiasm?

Now imagine yourself twenty years down that road. What's that like?

Here's why we asked these questions.

People don't buy books like *Clients Forever* because their business relationships are financially and emotionally fulfilling and they're experiencing connection and a sense of community. People buy books—and they sign up for workshops with people like us—because they sense that, no matter how good their business life is, it could be much better.

People buy books and attend seminars because they sense that, without change, their prospects for future success and happiness—for a rich, full business life—are constrained. They sense that their current path may not be the quickest route to the results they want, and they're worried about traveling any farther along it.

Your perceptions about the path you're on are accurate. Without change, you'll experience more of what you already know and have. That's the bad news.

The good news?

There's a fork in the road.

CHAPTER 2

WHY YOUR CLIENTS DON'T LOVE WHAT YOU DO

If you're like most people who sell for a living, you have some sales training under your belt. You've attended a number of seminars and purchased a few dozen books and tapes.

We'll bet you found true pearls in these seminars and books. *Wow,* you thought, *that's a good idea.* And, after turning the final page or shaking the last hand on your way out of the conference room, we'll wager you decided to adopt a new strategy or technique.

Put a rough figure on the amount of money you've spent in pursuit of the perfect sales system. We know of at least two sales professionals who've shelled out more than $40,000 of their own money and are willing to spend more. You probably haven't spent nearly this much. Perhaps your company has invested in sales training on your behalf. All told, how much money has gone into developing your sales career?

Factor time in, too. If you lump all the seat warming and page turning together, you might have spent a few solid months of your working life figuring out how to sell better.

Answering the next question might be painful. We're sorry if you wince; we'd make this point another way if we could.

How much of what you've learned in sales seminars, books, and tapes are you still using regularly?

Be honest with yourself. Come up with a percentage figure. We won't ask you to tell anyone or write it down; it's your secret. Be sure your answer is accurate, though. You might be tempted to inflate it because of what you've invested.

If you're like most salespeople, you haven't come close to making your investment pay off. Tracking a direct relationship between how much cash and time you've invested in sales training and their impact on your production is darn near impossible. If you could, though, and you were like many sales professionals, your return on investment would look pretty dismal.

Perhaps you think if you'd done something different your investment in learning new sales techniques and strategies would have paid off. If only you'd persisted, focused better, been more motivated or committed, . . . whatever.

There might be a small grain of truth here because pure activity *will* get you a result. If you do something, anything, you'll get a better result than you will by just sitting there waiting for the phone to ring. You might only get two sales for every hundred people you talk to, but you'll eventually get two sales.

However, read on before beating yourself up for not doing enough. If you're typical, it's more likely that you've been running down the wrong tunnel.

Books, audiotapes, seminars, rallies, interactive videos—the vast majority are about *doing* something different. Their promise? Do this and you've got 'em. *Establish rapport this way. Cultivate trust like this. Here are nine surefire ways to close. Probe for your prospect's pain with these questions.*

Your sales manager may reinforce the idea that you're not doing what you need to do in order to get results. You're not seeing enough people, closing hard enough. You need to work on your presentation. If what your sales manager did worked for her, she believes you need to do the same thing.

This is where we part company with nearly everyone else. The truth of the matter, as we see it, is that if you try to increase your production by *doing* something different, it probably won't work—for long.

DOOBIE DOOBIE DON'T

In fact, continuing to merely try to *do* things differently works against you.

Sales strategies or tactics you learn from someone else usually feel unnatural. You unconsciously tense up a little when you're about to employ them. Your position might shift, tension in your hands or face may reveal your discomfort, your voice might even rise or speed up a little. These aren't dramatic changes nor do they have to be for prospects to pick up on them.

Animals, including humans, are adept at sensing tension because it's a key indicator of impending danger. Your buyer, subconsciously aware of the shift in you, goes on the alert. You're the lion who's been dozing under an acacia tree, and your buyer is an antelope who just saw your tail start twitching. He or she bolts while you're still thinking about how hungry you are.

Here's the short version, minus The Nature Channel. If you're *doing* something to people, you know it and so do they. They don't like it. They run in the opposite direction. Clients who are running away don't love you.

🌿

CLIENTS FOREVER Wise Dictum Number 1
The more you copy someone else's style, the less effective you are.

🌿

WHAT HAPPENS OVER TIME

If you try someone else's best sales practice, the usual chain of events goes like this:

You get excited about a new sales tactic because it promises to fill a void in your effectiveness. You start out with a sense of purpose and good intentions. These techniques and strategies usually don't work right off the bat, though, because you're telegraphing tension to your buyer.

You could keep rehearsing and refining the technique by changing phrasing, inflection, or individual words. You might hope that it will eventually feel completely natural.

This may never happen. It's very difficult to make someone else's ideas your own. It's extraordinarily difficult to internalize something that wasn't yours to begin with and isn't a natural expression of who you are.

For example, we have what we think is the best referral process in existence. One of our coaching clients has gotten as many as fourteen names at one sitting—from someone who wasn't even her client to begin with. In Chapter 14, we'll cover the process in depth. We'll leave out the details for now; if you try it without going through the intervening process, it won't work. Suffice it to say that the process is predictably effective.

However, another coaching client of ours hasn't been able to make it work. For the first six years he was in business, he received four or five spontaneous referrals every week. Then this stream slowed, so soliciting referrals became more important.

We started by asking him how he used our method. Our words don't fit his usual syntax, so he'd twisted and tweaked them to make our approach a better fit. However, it still wasn't working.

Pretty quickly, we all realized there was something else going on. He believes it's not okay to ask for help; he's embarrassed. He could change the words all he wants, but the technique will never be his. As long as he believes he shouldn't ask for help, he'll tighten up—no matter what words he uses.

(So we're engaged in a process to alter his beliefs about what helping means—to him and to the person he asks. We believe that allowing someone to give assistance is an honor. When we deny someone the opportunity to help us, we deny that person the opportunity to be great, to rise above his or her personal concerns, and see what a difference he or she can make in someone else's life.)

Eventually, because it didn't fit him, he would have given up on the idea altogether. If you're like most salespeople, you, too, give up on other people's strategies. You may not make this decision consciously, but they eventually become just more items on your *to-do* list. *I should say this. I have to remember to do that.*

Exciting ideas turn into unmet obligations. Plans that once inspired you provoke nagging feelings of guilt—when you recall them. Yet you can't forget your good ideas and intentions altogether because you didn't complete them.

There's no business like unfinished business. It lives on and on and on. Remember the last time you didn't say or do something you wanted to? If you're like the rest of us, you've played the mental video, oh, 500 times or so. Eventually, you punch the Play button less often, but the tape is still rewound and ready to go.

Again, if you're like most sales professionals, you've accumulated a fair number of incomplete ideas about how to improve your production. Occasionally, you might think something along the lines of, *If I'd just do everything I know to do, I'd be really awesome.*

Rather than inspiring you to try harder, this thought bogs you down. Nagging feelings of guilt and twinges of remorse weigh on you.

In Chapter 1, we introduced you to your deep-sea sidekick, the squid. The squid feeds on guilt and regret because it adds to your unconscious connection between past results and future possibilities. The squid salivates when it sees another sales strategy coming. It gobbles up your initial excitement and savors your dwindled enthusiasm. And the squid belches and licks its tentacles while it reminds you that either you're a lost cause or sales training is.

The squid has got to go.
Ahoy there, Captain Nemo.

BEING, NOT DOING

We've laid out our case against learning other people's best sales practices. They probably haven't yielded the results you hope for. We're eternal optimists, though, so it's entirely possible that the next training you attend could bring long-lasting, productive changes to your sales career. However, we also always keep in mind that Albert Einstein once described insanity as "doing the same thing over and over again and expecting different results."

We suggest that your success doesn't come from increasing your knowledge of sales techniques and strategies.

🌿

CLIENTS FOREVER Wise Dictum Number 2
Your business and results change when you stop worrying about what you're doing *in the sales process and start working on who you're* being.

🌿

Whoa. That might sound like something you'd hear in a workshop where people were drumming, chanting, and wearing little crystals on various body parts.

Try not to let the word get in the way of the idea. *Being* is, like *love,* shorthand for a complex concept. We use it to refer to your unique character, personality, preferences, values, and deepest desires.

You probably express your intrinsic way of being more readily around good friends and trusted family members than around strangers. If you're like many people, you might feel free to laugh more (or only at the good jokes), be more honest about what you think, speak spontaneously instead of weighing each word, or act on gut instincts around close friends and family. These are just a few examples of how you're different, more *you,* with people you trust and like.

You probably also already have some clients with whom you're like this. And they—like your friends and family—respond to you positively because of who you're being with them, not what you're doing. You don't spend much time thinking about what you can get from or do to them.

Unlike most other sales trainers, we're not interested in helping you *do* things differently. We want you to *be* who you are at your best in your business, to be the same person with your clients as you are with the people with whom you have the most trusting relationships. You'll see yourself, your clients, and your business differently—and the results will astound you.

THE DATING GAME

An analogy will help you see the difference between being and doing.

Imagine you're single. You'd love to have an S(spouse), SE (spousal equivalent), or SO (significant other)—but you don't at the moment. Your evening plans include an event where other singles will be present.

Imagine the process you go through beforehand. If you're into single social life, this will be easy for you. Even if your dating history is as old as eight-track tapes, try to remember what it felt like when you were in the market for love.

You start by getting ready. You take a shower, shave your legs or trim your nosehairs, and put on extra-heavy-duty antiperspirant and just the right amount of cologne. Then you move on to your closet, where you choose an outfit that conveys the right message: available but not desperate, successful but not self-absorbed, easygoing but not irresponsible.

You might even practice a few suave opening lines in the bathroom mirror. *Do you come here often? Haven't I seen you somewhere before?*

You go to all this trouble because when you meet someone, you want that person to say "Wow!"

Let's say a certain attractive someone said just that, and jump forward a couple of weeks in your budding relationship. You phone or email, careful not to do it too early, too late, too much, or too little. You give tokens of your affection. You spring for lunch or dinner, choosing the place carefully. In other words, you try hard to do all the right things.

As for conversation, you develop interest in the things your flame finds fascinating. You avoid topics you think might be controversial. You gab about subjects you know nothing about. You chatter about subjects you think you know something about.

If the two of you date long enough, though, you must eventually follow the advice Mom gave you while you were dabbing on Clearasil before your very first real date: Be yourself. Only then does your relationship have a ghost of a chance to endure over the long run.

So, Bachelor or Bachelorette Number 1, what does all this have to do with transforming your business? You've just read a good description of developing a business relationship based on *doing* the right things.

When you're going to meet a new prospect, you pay attention to how you present yourself. You do many of the things you would before meeting a potential love interest: make sure your hair looks good, wear the right clothes, the right watch, a touch of a good cologne or perfume. You may even try out your opening lines on a colleague or in the rearview mirror on the way to the meeting.

Again, you want to make prospects say "Wow!"

If you make a connection and your prospect seems inclined to buy, you're careful about calling at the right times: not too early or too late, and never too much. You charge lunch or dinner to your expense account.

In terms of conversation, you cater to your prospect. Even though you get seasick in a deep puddle, you sound like Long John Silver while admiring the marlin in his or her office. You make an effort to avoid contradicting your prospect. And, when it gets quiet, you default to your most comfortable topic of conversation: your company's products, values, mission statement, and the like.

While we wholeheartedly endorse personal hygiene and believe in making good impressions, doing the right thing seems unduly important in both situations. It seems critical to say the right thing, be charming or upbeat at all times, feign a connection that doesn't yet exist, and hide your honest opinions.

There's one important difference, though. In the first case, you have to eventually be yourself to make the relationship work. You have such constant contact with your rapidly becoming significant other that you just can't fake it for long.

In business relationships, though, you can sustain a facade longer. You can hold back from speaking the truth as you see it. You can try to deploy the sales strategies you've learned to reel in another close. You probably have some clients with whom you feel more free to express your honest opinions, but they seem few and far between. Ultimately, maintaining a facade based on doing is what wears you down a bit, no matter how successful you are.

TRANSFORMATION, NOT INSPIRATION

Your good intentions and initial enthusiasm about a new sales technique often fade because inspiration is temporary. No speaker or author, no matter how gifted, can give you both an idea and the energy that will propel you through the systematic and sustained effort of keeping it in place. Even if you had the energy, you probably don't have time to reinvent the way you do things while continuing to earn a living. In the end, nothing changes very much or for very long.

Transformation, however, is permanent. No reinvention required. At Clients Forever, we begin by helping you take apart the connection between your past experiences and your future possibilities. Starting with what's already inside you, who you are at your best, we delve into areas that may not seem directly related to sales or production. Trust us, they are.

The process is sequential; each exercise and idea builds on the preceding ones. You'll get far more from this book if you read the chapters in order, instead of skipping ahead.

To reduce that temptation for you, we'll tell you now how *Clients Forever* ends. You're sure of what's important to you, and your business practices speak volumes about your values.

You regard the sales process and your clients in a completely new way, and you become part of a whole community of people who live financially and emotionally rewarding lives.

What we propose is nothing less than a total revolution in the way you operate in the business world. That may seem like a tall order. But, in many ways, our job will be done by the time you turn the last page of *Clients Forever*.

STEP 1

Let's start with a seemingly unrelated but very-much-to-the-point story. We were in New Orleans a couple of years ago. Down in the French Quarter, some street performers—acrobats—completely captivated a crowd. Four short guys in their mid-twenties who looked like they worked in a Kwikmart had 200 people eating out of their hands.

At the end of a highly entertaining show, it was time for the final trick. They asked for thirteen volunteers and lined them up on their hands and knees on the sidewalk, shoulder to shoulder. One guy on either end started yelling, "Clear the sidewalk! Clear the sidewalk!" Spectators vacated the pavement. Picture thirteen people kneeling on concrete in the middle of New Orleans, wide open sidewalk at either end.

Hundreds of people were now watching. A bus even stopped. All of a sudden, we heard the sound of someone running very, very fast as one guy raced directly toward the thirteen kneeling people.

This is what went through our minds: *We know what he's going to do. He's going to leap over all thirteen people, land on his hands, do a front roll, a handspring/roundoff combination, and finish standing.* We thought, *Woohoo! That would be great!* We would have been impressed. We were ready to be impressed if he only hurt a couple of people at the very end of the line.

Here's what really happened. The guy did leap over the backs of the kneeling people. Like Superman without the cape, he was parallel to the ground, hands and arms outstretched. In the middle, over person number 6, he did what appeared to be impossible. Even though he was fully stretched out, he tucked and did a flip. He then came out of it and landed on his feet at the end.

The crowd went wild—and the four guys walked around with big buckets. We'll bet they cleared at least a couple hundred dollars just off the last trick.

After a few seconds of utter shock, we thought this: *Did we really see what we thought we just saw?* It was so incredible that we had to check with other spectators to verify the evidence turned in by our own eyes.

Let's look at why that was so profound—and why we took the time to tell you about some street performers in New Orleans. Our past experience with acrobats influenced what we expected and made us doubt what we'd seen. We never imagined a flip over person number 6 and would have said it was impossible. Before he did it, our beliefs about what humans could do eliminated it as a possibility.

What does this have to do with you? Everything. Your beliefs about the way the world works determine what you think is possible. And what you think is possible dictates your results. As far as we know, this is the case for every one of us. If you don't think something's possible, you aren't going to try. You may go through the motions, but you won't commit. (Imagine the acrobat thinking, over the back of person number 2, *Nah, this probably won't work.*)

The guy doing the flip represents you having a business life— a life—that you love: extraordinary clients, the time off you want, no marketing costs because your clients build your business for you. If your clients absolutely loved you, your business might not be a party. It would just feel like one.

Based on your past results, you may not believe it's possible. Those limiting beliefs could keep you from even trying. So we'll start right there. Let's look at the beliefs that could be limiting for you.

What do you believe that, if it were true, would make it impossible for you to work only with extraordinary clients who build your business for you, giving you a life you love?

Use the following exercise as an opportunity to explore what you believe about the nature of your business and industry, as well as what your beliefs are about the basic truths of being in business. Write down everything that comes to mind, no matter how invalid or ridiculous it may seem on the surface.

The following are some beliefs that workshop participants have mentioned. If you agree with any of these, restate them in your own words and add them to your list.

I can't afford to let go of my existing business.
There aren't enough people like my ideal clients in the market.
It might work in a different market but not here.
There's nothing in it for my clients to build my business like that.
Selling is like shaving; you have to do it every day.
You can't make everyone happy.
I can't compete with a well-known firm.
I don't know how to have those kinds of relationships with clients.
Greed and fear are the only things that motivate people.
There's not enough time.
Nobody refers to a prospect more powerful than they are.

Your turn now. What do you believe that, if it were true, would make it impossible or highly improbable that you could work with extraordinary clients who love you, build your business for you, and give you a life that you love?[1]

---

[1] At this point, let us remind you that you made a threefold promise in Chapter 1. Among other things, we asked you to do the exercises. Here's the first one—the equivalent of the acrobat making sure to double-knot his shoelaces. If you're going to try the flip without taking care of your shoelaces, we're not responsible. We're not even going to hang around to see what happens.

This would never work for me because . . .

STEP 1, PART 2

Now we'll shift focus a little bit. The next question is similar to the preceding one, but more personal in nature. Take a short break if you need to, so you're refreshed as you tackle this topic.

Think back on the last business meeting or gathering you attended. Let's set specific agendas aside for the moment. Underneath the surface, most people there basically wanted three things: to look good, sound smart, and radiate success.

Most of us cultivate a subtle swagger. We don't tell people about how things aren't working or what we think our weaknesses are. We hide them and put on a masterful facade that says, *Hey, I'm doing all right. Business is great. I sign autographs after four o'clock.*

And yet, for most of us, a little voice beneath the confident veneer whimpers, *Oh, geez, if they only knew. If they only knew what I/my business was really like they'd laugh/be disap-*

pointed/not accept me. The funny part is that we each think we're probably the only one with a little voice. Everybody else looks so good—except for that guy over there—they really *must* have it all together.

One thing is true. No matter what position we occupy, whether we wear Armani suits or overalls to work, we're all made up of many strengths and a few perceived weaknesses.

Notice the word *perceived.* It's key. As far as we know, we all believe that some aspects of our personality or style are liabilities, qualities we must overcome or control in order to succeed.

Please get personal with yourself and complete the following statement as many times and in as many different ways as you can until you run out of reasons why your business couldn't be built for you by your extraordinary clients, giving you a life you love. We'll just step into the hall while you take a personal moment to jot down what your little voice wants you to believe.

Feel free to use pencil, write lightly, and erase later if you're concerned about revealing your innermost thoughts. What's important about this exercise is going through the process of writing your answers down, not leaving them here for all eternity. If you worry someone will see them, you're less likely to be completely honest with yourself.

We don't ask workshop or seminar participants to share this information, but our personal coaching clients have talked about this. Here are some of the answers that have come out in one-on-one conversations.

It takes too much time to have all my relationships like this.
I couldn't handle having more people in my life who I'm close to.
I'm too old/young/unattractive to have extraordinary client relationships.

Only men/women know how to have those kinds of relationships.
I'm too shy/reserved/awkward.
I don't like many people.
Not *many people like me.*
I don't deserve to enjoy my work/succeed financially.
I'm not good enough.

Your turn now.

My business couldn't be built for me by extraordinary clients, giving me a life that I love, because . . .

This isn't therapy. It doesn't matter where your beliefs came from. What matters is that you recognize they're there.

START BY ADMITTING YOU'RE IN DENVER

You're just a few pages into *Clients Forever* and we're asking you to bare your soul. Granted, we're only asking you to bare it to yourself, but still . . .

We don't pose these questions lightly. There's a simple, legitimate, and compelling reason why we asked you to consider these beliefs about yourself and your business.

🍃

CLIENTS FOREVER Wise Dictum Number 3
You can't move out of a position you refuse to admit you're in.

🍃

Think about it. Imagine making travel arrangements to get from Cincinnati, Ohio, to Orlando, Florida. You lined up a great fare, and you're looking forward to visiting Disney World. There's only one problem: You're in Denver. For some reason, you're either unaware that you're 1088 miles away from your departure gate or unwilling to disclose this fact to the person booking your reservation.

You can act like you're going to Orlando all you want. You can pack a bag, go to the Denver airport, and stand in line with everybody else, but you aren't going to get to Orlando. In fact, you won't even get on a plane.

As you plan to move your business to a new level, your answers to the previous two questions provide you with your current coordinates. A few things that you believe about yourself and the nature of your business or industry define your present position. If you can't or won't get honest with yourself about your limiting beliefs, they can continue to exert the same potent influence that they have up until now. And you'll continue to be unaware of their impact.

You may also have some beliefs that will make it easier for you to transform your life and business. We haven't asked you about these yet. The first step is to deal with your limiting beliefs.

Misconceptions are like mold. They thrive in dark, moist spaces—and the inside of your head is perfect. Your brain is a hothouse for the explosive growth of counterproductive ideas. Fortunately, controlling this rampant proliferation is surprisingly easy.

Misunderstandings tend to wither when you move them out of your head. One way to do this is to write them down, as we've asked you to do. That way, you can keep the truth about what you believe just between you and the pages of *Clients Forever*. Beliefs that run counter to what you really want also wilt when you describe them to someone else. They just don't stand up very well to the light of day.

Interestingly enough, you can't get rid of these beliefs by focusing on them. People work on their little voices all the time. Fiercely disciplined people try to eradicate them, to no avail. Simple common sense tells you this is so.

For instance, no matter what you read in the next two seconds, don't think about your right leg. Thinking about your right leg is the single most destructive thought you can have right now. Whatever you do, think about anything except your right leg.

You blew it, didn't you? You thought about your right leg. In fact, in order to try *not* to think about your right leg, you had to think about it first. You mentally identified it as the thing that you weren't supposed to think about.

The same is true of your misconceptions. If you're striving to eliminate them, you have to remember what it is you're trying to forget. The very act of remembering perpetuates these beliefs, despite your intentions.

THE RED MUSTANG SYNDROME

At this point, let's take a satire break. We'll reconvene in three or four paragraphs.

Just make multiple copies of the following statement on index cards and tape them in your home and office, wherever you'll see them throughout the day. Your bathroom mirror is a good location, as is your computer monitor.

All my clients are extraordinary.

All you have to do is remind yourself to think good thoughts, and your whole life will change! *I'm good enough, I'm smart enough and, by golly, people like me.*

In fact, this would be an excellent time to get to work on any other problem areas in your life. Create some more cards while you're at it. *I'm wealthy and attractive*, for instance. Or *everyone loves me.* To cover every contingency and save time, you could just go with *I'm perfect in every way and I have everything I could ever want.*

Thanks for being back on time.

We couldn't resist poking a little fun at affirmations. While the power of positive thinking is immense, you need more than three-by-five cards.

You can't just override self-defeating beliefs. That's about as effective as standing in the Denver airport and insisting, ever so cheerfully, that you really *are* in Cincinnati. The only thing you'll get is the chance to try on a jacket with really long sleeves.

Instead, please consider that the lists you created are your personal red Mustangs. You can drive for months without noticing a single red Mustang on the road, but the minute you start thinking about buying one, they're everywhere. Your brain starts filtering the evidence around you in a new way.

Your brain excels at filtering evidence. You believe that you, your business, or your clients are a certain way, and your brain filters the evidence around you so that your beliefs are substantiated.

This is, by the way, a very handy trick on your brain's part. Recall the story of the acrobats. Because what we *saw* contrasted so sharply with what we *believed*, it took us several minutes to recover full cognitive capacity. Your brain lines up your perceptions with your beliefs so you don't have to walk around all day with your mouth hanging open and a vacant look in your eyes.

If you think you need as many clients as possible, you'll notice people who are prospecting all the time, shaking every hand and working each connection. If you think your clients don't really like you, you'll notice when they're distracted, busy, or stressed and take it personally. If you believe you're inarticulate, you'll be acutely aware of every conversation in which the right word eludes you.

The problem with red Mustangs is that they demand so much of your attention. While noticing four red convertibles on your commute home, you don't simultaneously pay attention to the white Camrys and green Explorers. You think of other subjects—tomorrow's meetings, tonight's game, your dinner plans—and absentmindedly count red cars.

However, as you pull out of the parking lot at work one evening, you decide to notice all three kinds of cars on the way home. In that case, you'll override your brain's filter and spot all three models.

Our point? Unless you make a *conscious decision* to notice something else, the road in front of you will seem full of red Mustangs—or, in this case, all the reasons that your life and business can't be what you want.

HIGHER LEVEL KNOWLEDGE

To transform your business, you have to notice something other than the same old red Mustangs. To do that, you have to literally change your mind. And to do *that*, you have to know a little bit about how you acquire beliefs. In other words, you have to know how you learn.

Most of us believe we know at least a little bit about the way life, business, and people are. (Some people think they know everything; this transformation will be much harder for them.)

We've learned these tidbits by living, also known to some people as the School of Hard Knocks.

Not surprisingly, since we all experience life differently, we learn different things. For a simple example, imagine you're standing on a busy corner in any large city in the country, waiting to walk across the street. In front of you, two cars collide in the middle of the intersection. Several dozen other people on both sides of the street also see the accident occur.

Now, imagine it's a slow news day—a *very* slow news day. Bored reporters have been sitting around with their feet on their desks, listening to the police scanners. This accident is the first interesting event all day, so five or six rush down to the scene within minutes.

They interview thirty bystanders. It's highly likely that they hear thirty different accounts of what happened. Each bystander sees the same event, but his or her account of it differs slightly. And each would be willing to swear that his or her version is what really happened.

This is *reality by experience*. One of the most powerful ways we believe what we do is because we've had some kind of direct contact with it.

We're usually content to stop right there—with our personal experience. You could be content to do that, too, except that you have another project in mind. You're wondering how to have a business—and life—you love, built for you by extraordinary clients. You have to take another step along the road of learning.

In our workshops, we bring a chair front and center and ask someone to demonstrate its use. First time, every time, someone comes up and sits down. We've all had experience with chairs. Duh.

This is where the subject might end, but not for us.

We then ask participants to come up with alternative explanations for the object in front of them. The first few are often pretty tame—ladder, stepstool, clothes rack—before creativity really kicks in—exercise equipment, dancing partner, lion tamer, murder weapon, window breaker, firewood, float, and so on. Once the possibilities come up, it's easy to imagine how they'd play out (although we're still mulling "float" over).

One question makes the difference between the first explanation and the last ones.

What else could be going on here?

The answers come from imagination. Your imagination is a powerful tool. Breakthroughs of all kinds occur because people imagine new scenarios.

BACK TO SCHOOL

If you're like many sales professionals, up until now you've focused on learning more about sales strategies and techniques or other people's stellar pitches. The first part is correct—you do need to learn more.

But not about sales. To transform your business, you need to learn how to make distinctions. According to behavioralists, making distinctions is one level of learning up from generalizing.

Take the chair from our previous example. A toddler would identify it as a chair. An older child or teen, at a higher level of learning, would distinguish between a wooden chair, an office chair, an armchair, and a bar stool. An antiques expert would make even finer distinctions about construction, origin, and age.

Notice we use the word *expert*. One of the hallmarks of an expert is the ability to make much finer distinctions than the majority of people can. Pick any subject—computers, foreign policy, wine, investments, health, cars—you name it, and experts know so much that they can discern very fine differences between members of the same category.

Unfortunately, if you're like most salespeople, you generalize about the sales process, buyers, and your industry far more often than you make distinctions. You notice similarities, not differences.

Go back to your first list of beliefs about why your clients can't build a life for you that you absolutely love. They represent the boxes into which you sort people and experiences. They're the holes where the pigeons of your business roost. Unconsciously, you immediately find ways in which each new client or situation is similar to the beliefs you listed, slip the experience into the right slot, and stop thinking.

You've just generalized. You could—and often do—stop right there. And that's exactly where you need to ask the question to learn something new.

What else could be going on here?

BACK TO BEING

The first subject we'd like you to ask that question about is sales itself. Imagine you're talking to a prospect, engaged in your usual process. Things seem to be going well, and you're probably going to get the sale. You might have a stray thought or two that runs along the lines of, *I must be doing OK here.*

At the end of the appointment, you remember something you did or said that seemed to work particularly well and make a mental note to try it again.

The next time, though, it falls flat. You think something like, *Great, another strategy that only worked once.* This is generalization in action. You just crammed another item into your ever-expanding mental file of tactics that don't work consistently.

This is the point where you can't stop thinking if you're going to transform your business and your life.

Ask it. Go on, ask it.

What else could be going on here?

Now use your imagination. We realize you might be starting the engine cold, but turn the key and give it a little gas.

If saying and doing the same thing brings different results, maybe the outcome isn't about what you say or do. Let's leave out some highly imaginative options like astrological signs, malice, and the fact that your neatly trimmed goatee reminds your prospect of his bearded aunt.

It's you. More precisely, the outcome depends on who you're being.

If you show up as a salesperson, you'll get treated like one. It doesn't matter what you say; if you're being Stanley Slicklip of the Silver Tongues, you'll come across as a semi-sleazy, hardcore selling machine. If that's who you want to be, more power to you. Pass *Clients Forever* on, please.

In the first chapter, we asked you to consider the possiblity that your business could be made up almost exclusively of clients you think of as extraordinary. In this chapter, we've asked you to get clear with yourself about why you believe this couldn't happen for you. We've shown you how these beliefs both alter your perceptions and are based on your experiences.

It's about time to change them, don't you think?

CHAPTER 3

WHAT YOU KNOW ABOUT SELLING— AND WHY PROSPECTS HATE IT

You believe certain things to be true about the sales process itself. These may strike you as too self-evident to bear discussion.

Or they may seem so obvious that you don't recognize them. We like the concept of the unrecognized obvious. For instance, no matter what the temperature in a room is, it's always called room temperature. No one has to warn you against ironing in the nude. And if, as physiologists tell us, muscle burns more calories than fat, then how many calories does fat burn?

You just don't question certain things. However, transforming your experience of being in business is much easier when you're aware of your obvious and unrecognized beliefs about sales and where they came from. Let's take a look at how sales strategies have evolved over time.

For longer than you can imagine, we humans have sold each other various services and commodities. Of course, how we've done it has shifted dramatically over time. As far as we can tell, at least seven generations have emerged throughout the long history of sales. Each one seems to appear as a result of a broad sociological shift.

MEET THOG, THE FIRST SALES PROFESSIONAL

Somewhere in dim and distant history, the first transaction between early humans took place. No one can know the exact circumstances. We're going to use our imaginations, though, and we don't expect an invitation to the Forum for Prehistorical Accuracy.

Picture a hairy being with a low brow and long arms. This is Thog; imagine him chomping on roots and berries in the gathering dusk. Normally, he'd wander and eat until he filled his belly and saunter back to his small band of companions empty-handed. That very day, though, Thog and the rest of the group escaped a sabertoothed tiger.

Unfortunately, Thog dropped his club while running for his life, and he knows that being clubless is a significant primeval liability. Thog also knows that his bandmate Grok can't forage because he hurt his leg during the escape. It's an every-hominid-for-himself world out there, though, so he doesn't particularly care that Grok will go hungry tonight.

That's not why he keeps gathering roots and twigs past the point of filling his stomach. Tonight, a radical concept percolates up through Thog's prehistoric brain, like water rising to the top of a bog.

He returns to the shelter of a Stone Age cliff, where Grok slumps, wincing, against a rock. Thog picks up Grok's club and offers the extra food.

Grok is quick on the uptake—and the first deal in human history is done. Trading is the first generation of sales. Fortunately, you don't need language to make someone else understand you want to trade one thing for another, as millions of passport-bearing, Bermuda-shorted Americans can attest.

A BIRD IN THE HAND

In the first sociological shift that affected the way you now make a living, prehistoric humans settled down. No longer nomads, they could capitalize on the power of controlling access to commodities.

Let's say the tribe of Thog's great-great-etcetera (you get the drift) grandson lived by the flint mother lode. Other local groups could search for their own sources or make their lives easier by trading. Then, as now, the promise of an easier life is a compelling reason to buy.

Second-generation sales depend on buyers seeking out sellers who offer desired goods. Any locality-based sales process, from grocery stores to automobile dealers, represents second-generation sales. If you offer a product or service that isn't generally available elsewhere, second-generation sales is working for you, too.

TAKING IT TO THE STREET

In the third generation of sales, sellers took commodities on the road. Peddlers are a classic example of third-generation salespeople. And, while it was possible to sell some wares on foot, transportation made it much easier.

Because they were more mobile, sellers could reach more prospects—but they also had to find them. Sellers knocked on crude doors and shouted or sang while approaching settlements. Later, they wheeled their goods down streets in bell-hung wheelbarrows and stood on corners holding signs. All these early forms of advertisement shared the same premise: If sellers don't let prospects know they exist, they won't make a sale.

Today, third-generation sales systems depend on constant prospecting. The rule seems to be *pitch, pitch, pitch*—in person, over the phone, through the mail, with infomercials. Many insurance sales systems are spinoffs of peddling, as agents constantly search out new prospects.

I'M BA-ACK!

The fourth generation of sales took the form of a route and was made possible by the Industrial Revolution. Independent farmers and artisans flocked to cities, becoming employees dependent on pay packets. For sellers, prospects became both more concentrated geographically and more likely to buy at certain times.

In financial services, debit agents provide an example of fourth-generation selling. They went door-to-door each payday, collecting premiums. A contemporary, more common, and less obvious example of this sales approach is cross-selling. Once you build a book of business, you turn to it first when your company comes out with something new. Your life insurance customers make easy prospects for annuities, for example. You go right back to your existing clients—the equivalent of a sales route—to sell them new products.

Any sales strategy involving continual contacts with the same client base is a form of route-based, fourth-generation sales. Stockbrokers provide another example. They may sell a good investment to a hundred people, then "drip" on them periodically about additional products and services.

A third example of fourth-generation selling takes place in the banking industry. The average bank customer uses only 1.8 of the twelve to twenty services a bank typically offers. Banks, however, understand that customers who use fewer than three services aren't captured clients. So they continually send out statement stuffers to entice their account holders to use more services.

Fourth-generation sales, like its predecessors, pertains to

finding buyers. The strategies developed in each of the first four generations can work together easily—and often do. Many sales professionals use a combination of serendipity, controlled access to a product or service, prospecting, and recontacting existing clients to find new business.

While the first four sales generations present different models for tracking down prospects, the next three suggest ways to proceed when you're in the presence of someone who might buy. By the way, it took about a million and a half years to get from Thog, Grok, and a handful of berries to statement stuffers from your bank. In contrast, the fifth, sixth, and seventh sales generations arose in less than a hundred years. We don't know what this development means, but we think it's interesting.

I KNOW WHAT YOU NEED

As the freight train of scientific discovery gained speed in the twentieth century, sales hopped on board. Fifth-generation sales is called the *scientific approach*. It's also known as *need-based selling* and developed, as far as we can tell, in 1939.

Fifth-generation sales systems are based on presentations. Certain actions and phrases are virtually guaranteed to bring results: *Do these things and you've got the sale. Find a prospect's need and fill it.* Fifth-generation sales is about approaches and openings, features, benefits, and evidence, along with tie-downs, nail-downs, hold-downs, or pin-downs. It's about responding to objections and rebuttals and 119 classic closes.

If you've ever attended a formal sales training, you probably learned fifth-generation, need-based selling. It centers on a presentation by a salesperson, and it remains the foundation for nearly every sales program taught today.

MR. NICE GUY

In the mid to late 1960s, a shift took place in sales that roughly corresponded to the enormous social upheavals of the time. Potential customers started saying things like, "Wait a minute. You don't know enough about my situation to know if your product will actually help me. You need to find out more about me and what I need before you start trying to sell me something."

Sales managers and trainers developed consultative—sixth-generation—selling in response. The notion behind this kind of selling is that the salesperson puts the client's needs first. You become an assistant buyer.

Instead of just delivering a presentation, you now punctuate it with questions. The answers tell you which part of the presentation to give next. Consultative selling methods emphasize building rapport, talking in terms of your prospect's interests, and trying to understand the situation from your prospect's point of view.

If you're like many salespeople, you use a fifth- or sixth-generation sales strategy, along with one or more of the first four strategies. You find buyers in certain ways and you move them toward a sale in certain other ways.

These strategies have been around for so long because they work. Some work extremely well—when they're the right match for the person using them; in other words, if they fit with his or her natural way of being in the world. People have built incredible careers on consultative or presentation-based sales. These are good strategies, but we've got something even better, easier, and more powerful.

Whether a sales technique arose in the sixth generation of sales or the first, it's based on the assumption that if sellers do the right thing, prospects buy. This premise should sound familiar by now. In the last chapter, we discussed how the emphasis on *doing* usually works against you. You know a strategy; your prospect doesn't. In the middle of a sales process, you think something like, *Now! This is when I use it!* You know in your heart that you're likely to win, and you tense up in anticipation. More often than not, your prospect notices, increasing the risk of a lost sale.

THEY'RE PUTTY IN YOUR HANDS

In each generation, first through sixth, sellers exercise power over buyers so they'll make decisions that are in the *sellers'* best interest. That's why you might sometimes feel as if you're manipulating prospects.

You are. Techniques for manipulating buyers have grown more refined. Yet the core assumption—sellers can and should influence prospects to buy—remains the same.

You don't want to manipulate anybody. (If you do relish controlling your prospects, you'll dislike Clients Forever. We don't know you, but we suspect the feeling would be mutual.) But, if all your training is in fifth- and sixth-generation sales, you probably don't have many other tools in the shed. If you only have a hammer, all your problems look like nails.

Many salespeople figure that they have to manipulate prospects a little bit to make a living, even though it makes them uncomfortable. Many people believe, for whatever reason, that the only way to get someone to do something is to force his or her hand—or close to it. In workshops and coaching sessions, we frequently hear sales professionals say they feel like they're selling their souls to be successful.

When we move on to seventh-generation sales, you'll bid manipulation goodbye. First, though, it's critical that you understand how subtly seductive your current sales approach most likely is. Otherwise, you might be tempted to bring bits and pieces of your current sales strategy along as you move into seventh-generation sales—which won't work.

To understand how fifth- and sixth-generation techniques manipulate prospects, you only have to reflect on your personal experiences as a buyer. Check it out. Do you know if somebody's closing you? Can you tell if that person is using an alternate choice or minor point close?

Of course you can. So can your prospects, even though they might not know what a minor point close is.

How do you feel when somebody's closing you? Sometimes, if a salesperson is very good and you're sure you want the product or service, you can sit back and enjoy the process. More often, though, you're likely to feel pressured, stressed, sometimes trapped.

So do prospects.

You don't need to feel bad about the tendency to try to manipulate. Fifth- and sixth-generation sales are time-honored techniques, and you're only practicing what others have preached. We also don't want you to feel bad right now, because you'll have a chance to feel really bad in about five seconds.

Evidence suggests that the higher the value of the sale, the more likely it is that a buyer will have a long-term relationship with the seller. Would you want to have a long-lasting relationship with someone who pressures you? (In workshops, someone invariably makes a joke about spouses at this point. Personally, we're above cheap humor.) If your prospect feels pressured, you become someone to be avoided, even if you offer the right product at the right price, time, and place.

Prospects bolt from pressure or resent it if they cave in. This point, by the way, is the time to feel bad.

MR. NICE GUY HAS A MEAN STREAK

OK, you can stop now.

You may take offense at the statement that most, if not all, consultative techniques are manipulative. However, as much as consultative salespeople believe they're putting clients' interests first, their method indicates something different.

They rely on a presentation but punctuate it with questions designed to further their own understanding about a client or prospect. Whether the client understands what he or she wants is irrelevant. The goal of a sales professional using a consultative system is to completely understand what prospects want and why they want it. Probing questions serve to qualify prospects and gather information with which they can be leveraged later.

Statements like *I need to understand this in order to help you* are dead giveaways about whose interests are being served. As long as the purpose of the discussion is to answer questions in the salesperson's mind, the prospect's interests aren't coming first.

Although many conscientious sales professionals believe their job is to make sound decisions on a buyer's behalf, their livelihood depends on decisions that involve a sale. The bottom line for salespeople who use consultative systems is that they, too, have to close—sometimes when they're not sure doing so is in the prospect's best interest.

The most recent consultative techniques are even subtler forms of manipulation. Relationship-based approaches aim to increase the affinity that prospects feel with a salesperson. Like the ones that came before, these approaches focus on what to do and say. The goal this time is to make prospects like you better and trust you more.

Why? *So they'll buy.*

Being well liked and trusted are inherently admirable goals. However, cultivating these qualities for the express purpose of getting something from the very people who like and trust you is downright Machiavellian. For us, it's still an excellent example of manipulation.

We're done ranting now.

WHAT ELSE IS THERE?

Many sales professionals, if they've been selling for a while, have at least a little experience with what it feels like to put their own interests aside. One particular type of anecdote comes up regularly in workshops. Each participant who volunteers it shares different details, but, at some point, each says something very much like this:

> I knew I could make the sale, and I turned them down. It just wasn't the right deal.

Workshop participants uniformly describe this experience as one that they really enjoyed, using words like *freeing* to talk about it. Their faces light up when they tell us about these pivotal moments. They lost a sale—but they received a huge emotional and energy boost instead.

When sellers begin to let gut feelings or certain knowledge lead them and their prospects away from a sale, something shifts inside them. They no longer come from a position of economic need—no matter what their goals and production are. Their relationship to themselves—and, most often, to their prospects—comes before a sale. This way of being in the sales process feels good, and powerful, in a whole new way.

Yet most of the people who tell these stories also believe that if they were to repeat this experience very often, they'd go out of business. This belief is partially true; their sales career would end in a hurry if they turned down too many sales.

But they're only looking at what happened—at *what they did*. They're missing the most important slice of the experience.

They acted because of gut feelings or an innate certainty. They came from a position of economic plenty, no matter what their checkbook balance was. They put their relationships with themselves and their prospects first.

Sure, they walked away from one sale. The problem arises when they assume, on the strength of a single experience, that being a certain way in the world means losing many more sales. They think that the power of the experience came from walking away, not from who they were being in the process.

The sense of freedom, enjoyment, and power that our workshop participants describe is available to you, if not all the time, then a significant portion of the time. It's the cornerstone of the Clients Forever approach to letting your clients build your business for you, giving you a life that you love. And it starts when you stop trying to get clients to do what you want them to.

BUT, FIRST, A BRIEF MESSAGE FROM TWO SOCIOLOGISTS

If you recall, we linked the emergence of each previous sales generation to a broad sociological change. We believe that a similarly far-reaching change underlies seventh-generation sales.

Unfortunately, sociological shifts appear much more obvious in the rearview mirror. It's hard to distinguish between random events and trends that are still taking shape. We have a few ideas, though, about what might be changing in Western culture to make a new generation of sales inevitable.

The shifts that occasioned the second through fourth generations had to do with where and how humans lived. The emerging transition, like the ones that gave rise to fifth- and sixth-generation sales, pertains to how we *think*.

Some aspects of our changing culture have been documented by actual social scientists, not just a couple of fly-by-night business pundits with sketchy credentials. In *The Cultural Creatives: How 50 Million People Are Changing the World*, Paul Ray and Sherry Ruth Anderson document thirteen years of survey research on more than 100,000 Americans, plus more than 100 focus groups.

Their research focused on values and found that "a quarter of all Americans have taken on a whole new worldview." One out of every four adults in this country—men and women of all races, religions, and occupations—share beliefs and values that separate them into a unique, never before identified subgroup.

What's important to this segment of the population are values like authenticity, self-expression, and altruism, to name just a few. Lest you think that Ray and Anderson describe New Age flakes, be aware that these Americans tend to be solidly middle class and relatively well educated; we're talking managers and professionals here. The book itself is mainstream, selling fast enough in hardback to warrant a soft cover version.

Ray and Anderson's research focused on one aspect of this segment of the population: values. We expect that, as other sociologists focus on these individuals, a more complete picture of who they are and how they behave will emerge. However, even though *Cultural Creatives* doesn't paint the full picture of these individuals, it paints a very important part. Values are a key indicator of how people think and feel.

The benefit to you of this information—and why we brought it up—is knowing how Ray and Anderson's research results fit into the generational progression of sales. They found that a significant change in the way we think *is* going on in our society. Right now, roughly 50 million Americans—and an estimated 90 million residents of the European Union—are the evidence that it's high time for the next generation of sales to gain momentum.

SEVENTH-GENERATION SALES

Finally.

You might be thinking, *This better be some fancy-shmancy stuff after all this buildup*.

Good, it is. But not fancy-shmancy.

Seventh-generation sales is actually very simple. Not necessarily easy right off the bat, but very simple.

It's all about who you're *being* in the sales process.

That's it.

As we said, it's very simple.

And it's very difficult to talk about.

If seventh-generation sales, like all the previous generations, was strategy-based, we could tell you what to do. We wouldn't be shy about telling you which words to use and which you should avoid. We'd tell you who to call at what time. Heck, we'd even tell you what color underwear to put on if we thought it would help; we're that committed to your success, that thorough, and that willing to talk the truth.

However, our job is to help you show up differently in the sales process, to *be* who you are so fully that your clients find you utterly trustworthy and compelling. When you show up in a new way, they love doing business with you. In fact, they can't wait to refer their friends and family members to you. They take care of your marketing for you, making sure that the people they send are exactly the ones who will most appreciate and enjoy doing business with you.

So, while we can describe what seventh-generation sales is, we can't tell you how to *do* it. Later on, we'll suggest a few questions to ask potential clients. That's all we have to say about *doing*. The rest of what you do is up to you. The seventh-generation approach is a completely individualized and highly personalized way to be in business. You're the only one who will know how to put it into action for yourself. And you'll know most of that by the time you finishing reading this book.

A hypothetical example may help you understand the difference between the first six generations of sales and the seventh. Imagine you're in the middle of the sales process with a prospect. You've asked all the right questions and you fully understand exactly what your prospect needs or wants. You can clearly see how your product or service will help.

Your potential client, however, doesn't have a clue. If he doesn't make a connection between his current circumstances and the impact of your product or service, is your prospect going to buy?

No.

If you're trained in fifth- or sixth-generation sales, you default to a pitch, trying to give your prospect more information. If he just perceived the value of what you're offering, you think, the correct decision would be obvious. Of course, your presentation or pitch centers on the reasons *you* believe he should buy.

Your potential client, however, starts to back away because he's not hearing anything that addresses his reasons for buying.

He starts giving you put-off objections: *I need to talk to my spouse, accountant, lawyer, friend, banker, advisor, whomever.* Prospects use put-offs when they feel pressured.

In the best case, you agree to check back in a day/week/month/after the busy season. In the worst case, you're trained in fifth-generation sales, and you start trying one of those 119 classic closes you learned.

See the antelope run.

Now let's reverse our hypothetical sales process. Imagine that your clients discover that using your product or service moves them directly toward a valuable goal of theirs. It forms a bridge between where they are and where they want to be. You, on the other hand, only marginally understand the mental connection your prospects make. Will your potential clients buy?

Yes.

Most salespeople believe they know why their prospects buy. The reasons they give are based on their personal views of what's important in the world of sales: product knowledge, response times, and ironclad guarantees, to name a few. In fact, we've attended sales trainings where we've been told, flat out, that it was irrelevant whether prospects understand the benefits of buying a product or service.

Seventh-generation sales are based on the opposite assumption: Your potential clients' desire to buy a product or service increases in direct proportion to their understanding of its impact on what's most important to them.

Take a moment to digest that one. We said, "their understanding of its impact on what's most important to *them*." Them. Not you. You don't have to understand diddley squat for a prospect to buy.

We once met with a sales manager who believed he knew exactly why prospects bought the service his company sold. He instructed his sales team to hammer home two benefits of an audit defense service: tax savings and protection from the Internal Revenue Service.

When one of the sales crews implemented the Clients Forever approach, the crew's sales went up 31 percent *that day*. However, the manager insisted that crew members resume pitching the benefits he'd outlined. Not surprisingly, their results returned to the original level—and stayed there.

The following is a simple example that makes it quite obvious why focusing on *your* reasons doesn't make sense. Let's say you own an airplane and boat dealership. One morning, a prospect comes in and says, "I want to buy an airplane." Would you ever make the following reply?

"OK, but before I can sell you one, I have to tell you about our boats, too."

Not likely. But when you're busy steering prospects toward what you want them to understand, you do essentially the same thing. You make your airplane buyers listen to irrelevant boat blabber when all they want to do is buy that plane.

It seems so obvious. It is, in fact, an example of the unrecognized obvious. It's so darn obvious that it's our next dictum:

🌿

CLIENTS FOREVER Wise Dictum Number 4
Prospects buy for their reasons, not yours.

🌿

IT'S NOT ABOUT SALES

Seventh-generation sales is a whole new mindset for sales professionals. It's more of a revolution than an evolution, because the seventh generation isn't about selling at all. It's about buying.

We even dislike using the words *selling* or *sales* in conjunction with it. So we have a second name for this radically different way of looking at what happens between buyers and sellers. We call it *revelational buying*.

Some revelations involve God and flaming landscape materials. We don't mean that kind of revelation. We're talking about the ordinary revelations we all experience many times in our lives. You make a new connection, and your perspective shifts. Revelations—or, as we sometimes call them, epiphanettes—are often accompanied by phrases like *Ah-ha!*, *Ohmigod!*, and the ever-popular *Eureka!* Inside your brain, it feels like Tab A just slipped into Slot B for the first time.

When prospects have a revelation, they buy. In a flash of insight, they build a new mental bridge between their paramount goals and a product or service. Then they feel compelled to take a step toward making the connection real. Prospects literally sell themselves.

You're not there to pitch or present, nor are you there to probe. Whether you fully understand what your prospect needs or wants is beside the point. What, then, is your job as a sales professional?

Your role is to create an environment for revelation, a setting for insight. By cultivating an atmosphere in which your prospects can discover for themselves a new connection between what's paramount to them and a product or service, you let them sell themselves.

You listen far more than you talk. You ask a few questions. You remember that the only thing that matters is if your prospect discovers something new.

REVELATION VERSUS PRESENTATION

Let's change tracks for a moment to explore the notion of revelation a little further.

Please bring to mind the last time you sat in a classroom during a lecture. In your mind, relive the experience of taking notes, the feelings of interest, restlessness, boredom, curiosity, or drowsiness. Recall what it felt like for you to be the passive recipient of information that someone else decided you needed to have.

How many insights did you experience in that setting? You probably learned quite a few things, but how many Ah-ha! moments did you have?

If you're like most of us, not too many. You may have found the information intriguing or even inspiring, but you probably didn't put things together in a whole new way during a lecture.

You might have occasionally felt on the brink of a new connection. Unless you were extraordinarily lucky, though, the lecturer kept talking, and you lost track of your new idea before it became fully formed. Perhaps you recall feeling frustrated as a result.

You were more likely to experience an epiphanette if you had the chance to talk over a burning question of yours. You were even *more* likely to have a revelation if, in a private conversation, the lecturer happened to ask *you* a deeply meaningful and thought-provoking question.

Revelations and acquiring information are two separate concepts. Revelations percolate up from within, and being asked to listen to information while they're brewing derails the process. Put another way, if you default to a presentation for any reason during a seventh-generation process, you choke off the revelations that might be forming inside your prospect's head.

Trust us, we know how steeped you are in the benefits of the product or service you're selling. We know you have exhaustive product knowledge and we admire and respect you because of it. But, please, keep it to yourself unless your potential client asks—and then keep the information to a minimum.

CLIENTS FOREVER Wise Dictum Number 5
Revelations stop when presentations start.

IT'S LIKE TEACHING A KID TO RIDE A BIKE

You can't give somebody else a revelation. You can only create an atmosphere in which one is more likely to occur.

If you've ever taught a child to ride a bike, you know the difference between trying to create a revelation and letting a revelation happen. As far as we can tell, a couple of approaches can be used to teach a kid to ride a bike: long-winded explanations and running alongside a teetering two-wheeler.

If you prefer the first style, you start out by explaining the mechanics of gravity and balance, pedaling and braking. You critique trial runs, suggesting ways that the child could have dealt with various problems that arose. As the child sets out again, you run alongside, madly shouting instructions. "Keep pedaling! Keep the handlebars straight! Go faster!"

Sooner or later, though, you realize that the kid can't follow your instructions. He or she is so intent on a personal internal process that what you're saying barely registers. The only remotely helpful thing you're doing is running alongside the bike.

So you stop trying to *teach* balancing. Instead, you just run alongside the bike, creating the conditions under which a child can experience the epiphany of balance firsthand. You trust the process and that the child will eventually get it.

MORE ABOUT REVELATIONS

Similarly, you want to create the conditions under which a prospect can have a firsthand revelation experience. You do it in the very same way—and you won't get nearly as out of breath.

You focus on what's going on for your prospect. Not what you think ought to be going on or what typically goes on or what would be going on for you if you were the prospect. Nope, you just sit there and focus on your prospect's discovery process.

Our experience is that very few salespeople know how to let clients experience these insights. In fact, the more you *think* you know how to do this, the more you're moving in the wrong direction.

Earlier, we said that we'd suggest a series of questions to use; these will both prompt and help develop your potential clients' revelations. Before we give you these tools, though, it's critical that you understand the intention behind these questions.

If you're trained in a consultative sales strategy, you're adept at asking questions. You use them to qualify prospects and to find out more about what they need and want. A few pages back, we launched into a short diatribe about how a consultative probing process is thinly veiled manipulation.

It may seem, on the surface, that we're suggesting the very same thing: asking questions to help you leverage your prospect. We're not. The questions we suggest later in *Clients Forever* have a purpose radically different from those you might use in a consultative process. They are to help *prospects* understand their current situation and how they'd like it to change.

Focusing on your prospect's experience means that your own ideas, opinions, advice, and needs have no place in the conversation. Your product knowledge will come into play—if it does—once your potential client is no longer distracted by the always-compelling process of personal revelation. The less you talk about yourself, the more your clients discover about what's most important to them—their present and future experiences.

Obviously, your prospects greatly appreciate being truly—instead of nominally—at the center of the conversation. We'd be willing to lay odds that very few of your potential clients have had this experience while interacting with a salesperson. They love it—and they can't wait to tell their friends and family about it.

It also works for you in very powerful ways. First, focusing on your prospect's revelation process makes clear to her that you are utterly trustworthy. You don't need to interject your own agenda or control the conversation in other ways. Second, because you withhold all unsolicited advice, you communicate to your potential client that you fully trust her to make a good decision.

Finally, clients act more expansively on their own inclinations than they do in response to information, suggestions, or requests from you. This point is an important one. You may be a little anxious about how fully trusting your clients to make good decisions might impact your income. It may seem that if you didn't press for the sale, your production would drop off.

The reverse is actually true. When prospects no longer need to resist even the subtlest pressure to buy, they actually buy more and more often.

We believe people are more likely to resist even the most fantastic ideas when they come from someone else. Maybe we're just extraordinarily contrary—or perhaps we've stumbled on one of the unspoken truisms of being human.

Check it out for yourself. We assume you have friends and advisors. How many of their great ideas have you immediately and fully acted on? (We don't mean the little ones, like going to a movie. We mean the notions that require an investment of time or money. They sound like this: *You ought to start exercising more/eat less/put away more money each year/pay your quarterly taxes on time/look for another job.*)

If you're like us, you might get around to the activity, after you mull it over for a while—or you might not. However, if *you're* the one with the great idea, you're more likely to act on it and sooner.

In a nutshell, here's this central paradox of the seventh generation:

CLIENTS FOREVER Wise Dictum Number 6
The more you focus on your prospect's revelation, the more likely you are to meet your needs and goals.

HOW TO RUIN A PERFECT DATE

In the last chapter, we drew a parallel between dating and prospecting to help you see the difference between being and doing. We'll pick up where we left off, with the two of you a few weeks into a promising relationship.

You're starting to think that this person might be the one. It's time to find out whether this relationship has the sort of potential you think it does. Will the two of you be an item or not?

A special dinner is in order. Of course, you plan it around the kind of food your date likes, not your personal preferences. He or she likes Italian food? Ideally, you'd fly the two of you to Venice or Naples—or have an Italian master chef cater an intimate meal. If that's beyond your budget, you locate the best restaurant in the area or spend hours shopping and cooking.

Instinctively, you know that's one way to communicate how much you care about what's important to your potential partner. If he or she mentioned liking the way you look in a particular color or outfit, you're sure to wear it. You genuinely care about what's important to the other person.

Let's say the magic evening has arrived and you're sitting at a table for two. You look your best; so does your date. The two of you smile at each other in the opening moments of what you expect to be a very memorable evening.

You clear your throat. "Before we go any further," you say,

"I'd like to take a few minutes to tell you a little bit about myself: my family, our background, what we believe about the way
relationships should work."

Ha! You'd never do this on a date, would you? (Or have you?
Perhaps this is why you're still looking for Mr. or Ms. Right.)

Now imagine that this is a prospect. Perhaps you initiated
the relationship; perhaps your prospect did. In any case, you've
built enough of a relationship to get to the critical moment. Will
there be a deal or not?

You might arrange to take your prospect out for a nice meal,
choosing a restaurant your prospect enjoys. You'd probably
have a few moments of idle conversation to re-establish your
connection. At some point, though, you'd be ready to get down
to business.

"I'd like to tell you," you might begin, "a little bit about my
company: our products and history, and what we stand for."

This scenario doesn't seem nearly as far-fetched as the other
one, does it? The good news is that steering the conversation
this way is less shocking to a prospect than it is to a date.

The bad news is that your prospects don't want to hear your
stuff either. They may smile politely while you blab, because they
expect you to show up as a salesperson. The truth is, though,
they're not yet interested in your products, services, guarantees,
track record, and so forth.

What are they interested in? The same things we all are. They
want to be treated in such a way that they feel good about themselves when they're with you. They want to have their thoughts
and beliefs validated, not violated. They want to know what
kind of a person you are, not what kind of products you sell or
how long you've been with the Whatsis Corporation.

A NEW MODEL

Here's an analogy that will tell you a little more about
seventh-generation sales. We're going to assume that you have

at least one friend. (We love going out on a limb.) Let's say you and your friend decided to meet for lunch one day. You're looking forward to catching up, sharing your news, and hearing what's going on in your friend's life.

As soon as you meet, though, you can tell something's up. Your friend has something on his mind. You spend a few minutes reconnecting with each other, but you know your friend is really thinking about something else.

The following is likely to happen. One of you would eventually get to the point. Maybe he says, "I've got a problem." Maybe you say, "So what's going on?" You don't script it in advance. You know you'll know when the time is right.

Then you listen. You let the full picture emerge in the way your friend wants to tell it. It doesn't matter that you had your own agenda of news you wanted to share; it can wait. You'd never shift the conversation to something other than what's on your friend's mind. You know he needs to work something out. Perhaps you ask a few questions to help him consider what he might be overlooking.

You make a point of not interrupting. One-upsmanship is also out of the question. The last thing your friend needs to hear is something that begins, "You think that's bad? Did I ever tell you about the time . . ." Nor do you minimize your friend's concern by saying something like, "I know exactly what you're going through."

As the conversation goes on, you gain a deeper understanding of what's going on for your friend, and your friend gains some insight from being able to talk about the situation. "I never thought of this until right now," he might say, or "Do you think it could be this way?"

You answer honestly. That's why your friend called you, because he wanted to know what you really think. You'd be shortchanging him and the relationship if you hedged your opinion. Also, he's speaking truth, and you don't want to answer with anything insincere.

Eventually, your friend talks himself out. After three and a half hours or thirty minutes, he's fully expressed himself and his concerns. That could be the end of it. Or maybe he's got one last question for you: "If you were me, what would you do?"

You have a couple of likely responses. You're not living your friend's life, and you want him to make the decision that's best for him. So, depending on the nature of the situation, you might say something like, "I can't make that choice for you, but I'll support you, no matter what. What can I do right now to help?"

Another response might be: "Well, if it were me, I'd do this and this and this. What do you think?"

The premise underlying *Clients Forever* is that you can have buying relationships like the friendship we just described. You show up fully ready to be there for your prospect's benefit, no matter what decision she makes. Your most heartfelt desire is for your prospect to experience a revelation, because you know that will help her move from where she is to where she wants to be. You also know you can't provide the insight—you can just provide the environment in which it might happen.

If your prospect asks your opinion, you answer honestly. Not only will your prospect know if you're concealing something, it's a disservice to both of you and your relationship if you're less than completely open. That's what your prospect craves from you—the honest truth. At some point in time, she'll want to know about what you do and how you do it to know if it will help her. But that information is only appropriate in response to her revelation.

Similarly, if, at the end of the conversation, your prospect asks, "If you were me, what would you do?" you answer with as much information as seems appropriate. If he or she doesn't ask that kind of question, you might inquire, "What would you like me to do at this point?"

Or it might be a natural extension of the conversation for you to say: "It sounds like this is the right path for you to take. If it were me, I'd do this and this and this. What do you think?"

Depending on the topic of the conversation, you might also say, "I can't make that choice for you, but I'll support you, no matter what. What can I do right now to help?"

You'll know which of these—or something else entirely—is best. By this point in the conversation, you've been so completely honest that you can't imagine dropping into a sales strategy. You know how it would feel, and you don't want to go there.

THANKS, MOM

Be yourself. It applies to your whole life, personal and business relationships alike. It's simple advice.

It may, however, run counter to the behaviors that won you the success you now have. Being yourself is the opposite of trying. You can't be more yourself by doing anything better or faster or bigger. You can't *act* like you being yourself, either. We're talking authentic, dyed-in-the-wool, honest, trustworthy you.

Trust us, being yourself is the most radically effective thing you can do for yourself, your business, and your future. It's the difference between having a career and getting a life, between putting in time to make a buck and enjoying the heck out of the time you put in, and between constantly looking for the next new client and having clients forever.

Being yourself can also be a big leap. Most people don't wake up one day, look in the bathroom mirror while shaving or putting on eye makeup, and think to themselves, *From now on, I'm going to be completely honest about who I am and what I believe.* If they do have that kind of a mental conversation with themselves, they often find themselves repeating old behavior patterns unless they do the necessary groundwork to support their resolution.

That's what we're here for. We know some steps that nearly all people need to go through before they can make their business life congruent with who they are as individuals. That's the process we'll take you through as you read on.

If you're a little concerned that we might get all touchy-feely on you, rest assured. We're not going to invite you to a group hug or bring out the box of tissues we've been hiding. No delving into your murky past or required poetry readings.

Well, except for the bit in the first chapter about Robert Frost and the traveler standing at a fork in the road. We bring that up for a good reason here. If you recall, the traveler realizes that once he starts down a path, he won't return to the fork in the road. The path he chooses will inevitably take him farther and farther away from where he started.

You're still reading—you've moved quite some way down the *Clients Forever* path already. To judge the truth of this statement for yourself, consider how your business might be different if you never read another word. We've introduced some powerful notions, the impact of which you would experience even if you decided to stop right here.

> *Prospects buy for their reasons, not yours.*
> *Revelations stop when presentations start.*
> *The more you focus on your prospect's revelation, the more likely you are to meet your needs and goals.*

We'd wager that these notions would affect the way you do business even if you decided to stop reading right here.

But keep going. To experience a life that you love, built for you by extraordinary clients, you'll want to go through the steps that help you be in business at your full, free, powerful best.

HAVE A LITTLE FAITH

It should be clear that trust fuels the seventh-generation approach. However, unlike other trust-based sales techniques, *you*—not your clients and prospects—have to do the trusting.

You have to trust the process of allowing prospects to sell themselves. You have to trust that they'll make good decisions for themselves—and that their decisions will also benefit you. You have to trust yourself enough to be quiet, instead of launching into presentation mode.

Whoa, Nelly. That's a whole lot of stuff to start trusting. We imagine you might be wondering, right about now, *How the heck do I cultivate enough trust to do this?*

You practice. Trust is both the end and the most effective means of reaching that end. Like a muscle, it grows stronger with exercise.

We'll help you cultivate trust with a series of simple exercises that allow you to better understand who you are. By the time you turn the last page of *Clients Forever*, you'll have a good sense of the answers to three key questions:

Who am I?
What's worth doing?
Who's worth being around?

As you better understand your way of being, you have a viable alternative to focusing on *doing*. You become able to get out of your own way in conversations with your current and potential clients. If you understand your way of being and what activities deserve your time and energy, you become better able to trust your clients to make good decisions. Eventually, you realize that they're capable of nothing less—and you measure your success by how effectively you've supported them in reaching and acting on intelligent, autonomous choices.

That's all very well and good for your prospects—and for your sense of personal satisfaction. However, if you cultivate the kind of self-awareness, calm confidence, and trust we've seen in seventh-generation sales professionals, the results get even better.

Your unshakable belief that your prospects have the right

answers for themselves and can be trusted to make good decisions is at the core of living a transformed business life. Earlier, we pointed out that prospects act more expansively on their own impetus than in response to your information, suggestions, and requests. You experience this as bigger and higher quality sales. Consequently, you can afford to stop maintaining clients with whom you don't enjoy working.

We also pointed out that, the higher the value of the sale, the more likely it is that clients want to have a long-term relationship with you. You experience this phenomenon as an increased client retention rate.

Your clients see their interaction with you as utterly unique, a friendship instead of another knot in a long string of first dates with salespeople. They can't wait to tell the other people in their lives about it. You experience this trend as more unsolicited referrals. Your marketing activities eat up less time because your clients send you more referrals.

One short word is the key to you experiencing a life that you love, built for you by your clients.

🍃

CLIENTS FOREVER Wise Dictum Number 8
Trust.

🍃

CHAPTER 4

ON TRUST

You might be the most trusting person on the face of the earth. That's no guarantee, however, that anyone trusts you.

No quid pro quo of confidence exists. Some people are so innately distrustful that they withhold their trust under any circumstances. For example, they keep money under the mattress because even the Federal Deposit Insurance Corporation seems suspect. Others trust only in certain circumstances or for reasons they're not aware of. Trust can be a one-way train. You can't demand someone's trust; that person has to give it to you.

Your way of being, however, can either engender or undermine trust in you on the part of others. Let's take a look at three cautionary tales about trust.

CAUTIONARY TALE NUMBER 1

A few years back, we were hired as consultants to oversee all the training programs for a great new venture at a gargantuan health care company. We conducted training for managers, inside sales staff, outside sales staff, group presenter sales staff, and several analysts. Once a month, we spent four days in a row with people whose job it was to sell the terrific idea to consumers.

The general manager of the venture had hired us. We'll call him Jim. He had impeccable credentials; after graduating from a top-flight M.B.A. program, he worked for one of the premier consulting firms in the country. Jim was brilliant—and a darn nice guy, to boot.

Over time, as we worked with the people Jim managed, we became aware of something that confused us. They thought the program was good, but they questioned whether or not it would ever get implemented. They were also convinced that the company would somehow botch things up.

On the surface, it seemed like the sales staff ought to have been eating out of Jim's hand. We used to teach six different ways to create rapport, and he unconsciously used them all. He was likable, friendly, and supportive.

Later, after the training was complete, we were called in for a special meeting on conflict resolution. At that point, we finally figured out what was going on. Jim's sales staff didn't trust him because he didn't have predictable, acceptable behavior—what we called PAB. In fact, unbeknownst to us, Jim's track record was so poor that he actually had the near-opposite of PAB.

For instance, the company's accounting system had been delinquent about cutting commission checks. Jim said he'd take care of it. Perhaps he tried to do so, but, by the time we came on the scene, some checks were more than a year late. Jim represented the company in his employees' minds, and their experience was that commissions were being botched up. The sales staff felt as though *they* weren't being taken care of, so they didn't trust the company to take care of its customers, either. No wonder they dragged their feet a little in the sales process.

Jim also had a history of implementing changes, then revising the plan before implementation was complete. Sometimes, he'd change the plan before the first set of changes were even implemented. No wonder the staff doubted that the new program would ever be put in place.

Jim's staff loved going to workshops with him. He was fun to be around. He was an incredible speaker. However, when push came to shove, his behavior wasn't predictable and his results weren't acceptable. They knew they couldn't trust him to stick with the plan he outlined.

The moral of the story? PAB is an important part of cultivating trust. This story speaks volumes about how important predictable behavior is to trust.

If you say something's going to happen, it had better happen. Two steps have to be in place before it does, though. First, you'd better know how to make it happen by having the basic competencies for the job you're doing. Second, you'd better follow through so it does.

Jim's employees didn't trust him. His lack of PAB was so stressful for them that, despite how much they liked him personally, they were relieved when he was eventually asked to leave the company.

Now, imagine they'd been clients, not employees. They would have left long before he did.

CAUTIONARY TALE NUMBER 2

Sue, a coaching client of ours, recently lost a client whose account was worth an annual $125,000 in income to her. Sue had had this client for ten years, and she lost the account very suddenly.

After moving his account to another financial advisor, Sue's client said, "You just don't seem like you have time for me anymore, so I'm going to try somebody else." His investments were fine. Something went sour in the relationship.

On reflection, Sue had some insight into what happened. "The last time I talked to him, I was systematically calling all my clients. He was just one of a long list of calls I had to make.

"My company is also changing in ways that are putting new stress on me. I feel tense, and he noticed that. I'm not the person he thought he knew."

The message of this tale is that predictable, acceptable behavior is about much more than job competencies. It's about how you relate to people, too.

Another point of the story is that, like beauty, acceptable behavior is in the eye of the beholder. Contact alone wasn't satisfactory for Sue's client; he wanted highly personal contact.

CAUTIONARY TALE NUMBER 3

Another client of ours, Bob, once hired a trust attorney. (This isn't an ironic twist we added for effect—it really was a *trust* attorney.) Bob was impressed with this attorney's mastery of trust law. He helped Bob create a family living trust, and Bob developed great confidence in the attorney's ability to handle any trust-related contingency.

Much later, Bob and his wife divorced. Bob called the trust attorney about rectifying the trust in light of his new circumstances.

The attorney laughed.

"You can't rectify it," he said. "You have to get a new one. In fact, you need a new will, too."

The attorney chuckled again.

"You no longer have a family, so you violated a basic part of the family living trust."

The facts were true. Just as Bob expected, he got sound advice from his attorney. However, the way that advice was delivered didn't work for him at all. The trust expert's inappropriate laughter and condescending tone of voice cost him Bob's business and any referrals he might have received.

This story reveals another element of the A in PAB. Relationships are built on acceptable and *accepting* behavior. In fact, acceptance is the foundation of revelational buying.

What do we mean by acceptance? Clients know that they're going to be OK with you. Like Bob, they can be vulnerable. However, unlike Bob, they're not hurt as a result of their openness. They can be fully themselves and receive approval and understanding.

HOW'S IT GOING SO FAR?

Your current relationships can give you an idea if your way of being is predictable, acceptable, and accepting. Have you noticed any stiffness or distance on the part of the people who are most important to you? It's important to pay attention to how others behave because the response you're getting from clients and prospects tends to be the message you're sending.

Clients and prospects generally respond to you in the same way you come across. If you're stiff or stilted, they'll be stand-offish or formal, too. If you protect yourself and hide the truth about what you really think and feel, they won't be any more candid than you are. For instance, you may notice that your clients and prospects answer your questions vaguely or evade them altogether. In that case, you can assume that they don't trust the truth of your response or they don't think your relationship is safe enough for them to give you an honest answer.

The more someone trusts you and your likely responses, the more specifically they answer your questions.

Take a moment and think about the people you're most ill at ease with while you're doing business. If you're like many of us, they tend to be people who are formal and reserved. While you may highly respect their skills and opinions, you probably don't express yourself as freely as you do in other circumstances. You're less likely to voice opinions that run counter to theirs or talk about mistakes you might have made. You're not alone. We all tend to be like the person we're associating with in the moment.

Now look at the flip side of this experience. Have you ever met someone who was so open and comfortable that you instantly felt at ease? If someone is relaxed, honest, and clearly comfortable in her or his own presence and with you, you probably feel more relaxed yourself. You say what you're thinking, instead of thinking about what you're going to say. You're more likely to answer questions and to do so fully and specifically.

In any given situation, we tend to key off the behavior of the most authoritative person. When you're the client, you attune your responses to the way of being of the expert across the desk or table from you. Your prospects do the same.

If you're being open, comfortable, and fully yourself, you create an environment that makes it possible for your clients and prospects to be themselves. They feel safe to be honest and open.

They probably won't do it right off the bat; they'll take some time to check out the situation, seeing if it's safe. However, as you're predictable and accepting, their experience will convince them that they can afford to be vulnerable with you. And they'll be absolutely right.

Sounds good, doesn't it?

You just have to be open and comfortable with clients and prospects. You don't have to memorize a list of predictable, acceptable ways to be: return all phone calls within two hours, send birthday cards to all your clients, nod in a certain way to show you're paying attention, and switch to the antiperspirant we recommend.

The only question left is this: How do you get to the point where you're comfortable with almost everyone you meet? The answer is: You get comfortable with yourself. And to do that, you get to know yourself and what's important to you.

SAME PIE, NEW SLICE

A while ago, we pointed out that, to make seventh-generation sales work for you in a way that transforms your business and your life, you have to trust a few things. You have to trust the process of letting your prospects sell themselves. You have to trust that your prospects can make decisions that are good for both of you.

What we've been talking about so far is how to cultivate a way of being that creates the environment in which your prospects are comfortable selling themselves. When you know yourself and what's important to you, you may also look at what's good for you in new ways.

Another item on the trust agenda is trusting yourself enough to be quiet, instead of defaulting to a presentation when there's a gap in the conversation. Self-trust is key to the whole process. It grows as you get to know yourself, helps you feel comfortable and ready to be open, and frees you from relying on a pitch or presentation.

TAKE A SYSTEMATIC LOOK

But, you might be thinking, *I trust myself implicitly*. That might indeed be true in some areas of your life. However, we've found that it's rarely true on a wholesale basis. Most of us rely on a few—or many—systems to make sure we don't screw up.

What do we mean by systems? Any method of doing things that you adhere to regularly. For instance, we have a system to keep us on track to meet writing goals; we've learned that we get behind schedule without one.

If you take a look at the systems you have in place, you'll get an idea of where you view yourself as less reliable. If you use three alarm clocks to wake yourself up, you doubt that, left to your own devices, you'd ever get up on time. If you rely on a formula sales presentation, you might not trust yourself to be spontaneous and still get the sale.

Systems can be simple: notes, clocks, appointment books. They can also be very complex. An acquaintance of ours runs a large enterprise. He's a charming guy, very personable and funny.

His company is also nearly paralyzed with accountability systems for his staff. The vast majority of their time is eaten up by staff meetings, sales meetings, reporting meetings, filling out reports, and so forth.

Clearly, this isn't the most efficient way to run a company. To try to make the numbers better, our friend continually re-designs how things work. In each of eight or nine versions, these systems have been variously and ingeniously cumbersome.

Here's the kicker: While we really like this guy, he's almost completely unreliable. His word means nothing—or close to it. His accountability systems are in place because he doesn't trust himself to do what he says he's going to.

THE TRADE-OFF BETWEEN CONTROL AND CHOICE

If you know that you can handle anything that comes up, you can afford to let other people act freely. In other words, if you trust your ability to deal with all—or nearly all—situations, you don't have to control other people's actions or decisions.

Most sales scripts have an alternate choice embedded in them. A salesperson sounds as though he or she offers valid alternatives; in reality, either choice steers the prospect in the direction the salesperson wants. *Would you rather have a leather interior or cloth? Would you prefer a traditional or a Roth IRA? Are you more comfortable with low-yield, low-risk investments or high-risk, potentially high-yield vehicles?*

What sounds like two options is really one. Prospects have to choose option B if they don't like option A and vice versa. They can't easily opt out of the underlying assumption—that they really want the car, the retirement account, or the investment. Offering two options funnels the conversation toward the salesperson's goal.

If you trusted yourself to deal with whatever your clients and prospects decided, you could afford to let them have as many choices as they wanted. The need to control things by offering only the illusion of choice is an indicator that you mistrust your ability to handle the unexpected.

MASTER OF THE UNIVERSE

If you trust your intention and ability to have grace under fire, you can afford to be wrong. If you don't, you can't.

We've been in training sessions where being right was one of the tools we were taught. People want to look good, we heard, and one of the ways you can look good is by being right all the time.

The problem with this scenario is that if you always have to be right, somebody else is probably being made wrong. If you're looking good by being right, unless your prospect agrees with everything you say, you have to make them wrong. If you're so important that you have to be the one with all the answers, the message you're sending is that your client is less important.

Most of us tend—at least a little bit—to feel like we have to have all the answers, limit other people's choices, or rely on systems to bolster ourselves where we feel weakest. None of these are heinous crimes, in and of themselves.

The difficulty is that neither are they consistent with seventh-generation sales. Prospects who are wrong or less important than the sales professional don't fit into a revelational buying process. If your prospect doesn't feel free to make any choice he or she wants, there won't be any epiphanette in the works. If you fall back on a presentation, you've just left seventh-generation sales.

The question then is: How do you increase your self-trust?

HOW TO TRUST YOURSELF

Kurt Wright, author of *Breaking the Rules: Removing the Obstacles to Effortless High Performance*, suggests that you learn how to trust yourself by sharing parts of yourself in an environment where you get validated. As that experience focuses on helping you discover things about yourself that you might not have been aware of, you get to know yourself better. You understand what's important to you. You're more comfortable with yourself and with everyone with whom you come into contact.

This can have tremendous power for you personally. It's very freeing to develop more self-trust and confidence as a result of having new parts of yourself validated rather than violated. Even without another goal in mind, becoming more comfortable with yourself and trusting yourself more is a great life goal.

However, you do have a second goal in mind. You want to apply this experience in a way that utterly transforms your professional and personal life. You don't just want to feel good. You want to have a life that you love, built for you by your clients.

In the next few chapters, you'll get a chance to experience exactly what we're talking about and see how it applies to seventh-generation sales. The more you follow the directions, the more you'll experience the results available to you. As we've said all along, the power of *Clients Forever* is in the exercises, so don't shortchange yourself.

By following the directions, you'll also experience exactly

the kind of environment you want to create for your clients and prospects. You'll draw on these memories as you begin to apply the principles of seventh-generation sales to your business. Your clients and prospects will benefit from the experiences you have during the exercises.

CHAPTER 5

READ ME FIRST

Let's start with the three most dreaded words in workshop history.

Find a partner.

If you were attending our workshop, you wouldn't have a choice. We'd watch to make sure that everyone was part of a pair. If you hunched down in your chair and studiously avoided eye contact, we'd find you and assign you someone to work with.

You're on the honor system here. Find a partner.

We conduct these exercises in pairs because it's the only way to experience what we're talking about. The process requires two people: one to talk and one to listen. If you went through the following exercises alone, you might learn something about yourself.

However, you wouldn't have the experience that you need to do two things: (1) take a giant step toward transforming your business and your life, and (2) learn how to create an environment where your prospects and clients feel validated.

Finally, if you still need a reason to follow the game plan, allow us to remind you that seventh-generation sales are all about relationships. You can't hide alone in the back row to learn about it.

Your mission is to find someone to help you with the next few chapters. Each of the exercises will take around a half hour to complete. You don't have to find someone to make a lifetime commitment here.

As you consider the various people you know as a potential exercise partner, keep in mind that you're looking for a good listener who's interested in helping you. Pick someone who is really in your corner and with whom you feel comfortable being completely honest. He or she doesn't have to be particularly close to you, either. Your spouse or partner might seem like a convenient choice, but that person is probably too invested in your thoughts and feelings to set his or her own reactions aside. You want someone who you can trust to listen quietly while you go through the exercises that follow.

The following are some people you can eliminate right off the bat: your ex-spouse, anyone you owe money to, anyone who owes you money, anyone you can fire, and anyone who can fire you. These people do not make good choices. Also eliminate know-it-alls, gossips, competitors, and aspiring business consultants.

If we've just eliminated your entire circle of friends and acquaintances, you can always call a priest, minister, or rabbi. Pay a counselor or therapist, if you need to. Give a copy of *Clients Forever* to a business associate (we are so selfless), then go through the exercises together.

Just find someone. Then have that person read the next section.[1]

🍃   🍃   🍃

HI, HOW ARE YOU?

(This section is for the person who's agreed to help you. You
can skip to the next chapter. Really. We'd like to have a private
chat with your assistant.)

So you're the helper, eh? Nice to meet you. Thanks for step-
ping in, because you're going to make a big difference in your
friend's life.

What's going to happen here is that you're going to ask your
friend a series of questions. The most important thing for you to
remember is that *there are no right or wrong answers.* Whatever
your friend says is fine, whether or not you believe or agree with
it. Just because it may not be a true statement for you doesn't
mean it isn't a true statement for him or her. We're relying on
you to be the best possible listener you can be, not judging anything you hear.

You're here to listen, not advise. If you think you have an
insight to add, don't. Hold all your comments on whatever
comes up. If you say anything about what you think or feel, your
friend is more likely to try to come up with words or phrases
that you'll like. He or she can't help it; it's just part of human
nature.

Be patient. It's important that your friend find the words that
express his or her experience. If you think it will help your
friend's understanding, you can clarify the meaning behind your
friend's words. However, your understanding is less important
than your friend's.

---

[1] We know that, despite everything we've said, you still think you can do the exercises on your own. That kind of thinking is why you are where you are in your business right now.

As much as you can, maintain an interested and neutral facial expression. Checking your email, rolling your eyes, or dozing off are out of the question, so be sure you're ready to give your full attention to the process before you begin.

Your role isn't very glamorous. You're going to speak far less than your friend does. However, you're absolutely essential to the Clients Forever process, and we're grateful that you're here.

Please return us to the person who asked for your help.

CHAPTER 6

JUST EXACTLY WHO ARE YOU?

Thanks for waiting while we chatted with the person who agreed to help you. For the next few chapters, both of you should read the directions for each exercise as you come to it. The easiest way to do this is to buy another copy of *Clients Forever* and give it to the person who's helping you. (We're only thinking of you.)

The exercises take a little more time from this point on. Figure on spending at least a half hour on each one—still not a huge amount of time to invest in radically changing your life.

TURN OFF THE COLD WATER

To make sure your investment pays off, you want to have a certain perspective. We'll start with an exercise that will help you have the most effective possible experience from this point on.

The directions are very simple. Write down everything you don't like or don't want in your life. You can do this in your partner's presence or before the two of you meet. When you're done, briefly tell your partner what you've written.

An explanation of why you're doing this is as follows:

Have you ever set a goal that you didn't achieve? Nearly everyone has had this experience, professionally or personally. Think of the last time this happened to you. Where did you intend to go and where did you end up instead?

In the situation you brought to mind, consider yourself to be a water faucet. When you're pursuing a goal, you need to run the hottest water you can. Take the governor off the heating element—you want steam billowing up around you and the windows fogging over.

If you're like many people, though, you ran lukewarm. You thought about running hot water, you talked about running hot water, but the cold-water faucet just kept dribbling, cooling down the mixture. If you're going to reach your goal, you need to shut it off.

You can't, though, without knowing what the cold water is. In the situation you brought to mind, what diluted the heat of your desire to reach your goal?

In all likelihood, it was something rather familiar to you. Your unique dribble of cold water is most likely a fear: either of a past experience or something you imagine might happen.

For example, if procrastination is a lifelong habit of yours, you've probably watched deadlines go by without doing anything. Or perhaps you've mustered up a hasty, full court press at the last minute. You'd probably like to avoid both of these situations but fear that they're inevitable. If important people in your life tend to be disapproving, you may have wanted to avoid their reaction. Procrastination and the fear of disapproval are both examples of aspects of your current life that could contribute a steady stream of cold water. Can you imagine the difference if you were rid of them? (Notice we mean getting rid of the *fear* of disapproval, not getting rid of the disapproving person. Your life will certainly be transformed if you spend the rest of it behind bars, but that's not what we have in mind for you.)

You may also project unfounded fears into the future. As far as we can tell, most of us are exceptionally skilled at conjuring up big bad things that *could* happen, even though they never have before. For instance, many people long to make a career change but fear that they won't make enough money to survive.

So what is it you *don't* want to experience that keeps dripping for you? Are you afraid of continuing to experience something you already do or of creating a ripe circumstance for something disastrously new? Knowing this slows the cold-water drip down, so the heat of you moving toward your goal won't be diluted by what you don't want to bring along.

Through this process, many people discover something about themselves that they didn't know before. Or maybe you knew it on some level, but not consciously. Bringing it front and center is part of coming to know yourself better.

Doing this exercise with another person is a step toward developing more trust. You may feel vulnerable as you admit there are things about your life that you don't like, and you get to experience being validated, not violated.[1]

Reflect on your personal and business experiences, past, present, and imagined future. Fully express everything you don't want. Words, phrases, or complete sentences are fine—whatever works for you.

The following are some answers from workshop participants

---

[1] Note to partners: It's a good idea to refresh your memory about your role before each exercise. Your accepting response is key to the whole process.

to stimulate your thinking, just in case you're having trouble identifying anything you'd like to eliminate from your life. And, if you do feel stumped, we'd like to meet you. You're the first.

failure
rejection
pain
poverty
uncertainty
stress
loneliness
confrontation
fear
no love
no sex

Be both specific and brief. Writing down what you don't want can take a few minutes—or an hour. Just make sure you feel complete with the process before you stop.

Stop reading now and finish both parts of this exercise—writing what you don't want and telling your partner—before continuing. Use the space below for your list.

Welcome back. What did you discover in this process? Were there any surprises? The good news is that you've identified miscellaneous negative thoughts and given them a place to rest—on a piece of paper—so they can stop rattling around in your unconscious mind. This simple exercise helps you turn the cold water off so you can concentrate on what you really want.

WHAT'S IMPORTANT TO YOU?

Now that you know what you *don't* want to take along as you move forward, let's find out what you *do* want to bring along. You'll move a little deeper into finding out more about yourself and what makes you tick. You'll also develop more trust in yourself and experience, in a different way, what acceptance feels like.

Many people talk about values. Our experience is that most people don't know exactly what their values are. The questions in the next exercise will tell you exactly what you most value in your life. When you know what's really important to you, you can make better decisions about how to spend your time.

In this exercise, you'll answer the question, *What's important about life to you?* If you don't use the form that follows, create something like it by writing the question at the top of the page and drawing a vertical line down the center.

List your responses to this question to the left of the center line. Use words, phrases, sentences, whatever comes to mind. This isn't meant to be an essay on life. Record your spontaneous answers to this question without laboring over them. Later, we'll look more deeply at each item.

Your responses may fall into a number of different categories. Some answers refer to tangible things, like transportation or having a roof over your head. Some things are more about relationships, like family or having a good marriage or children. Some people list spiritual qualities or ideas. Some people list things like fun or sex or love or affection. Some people list qualities like integrity, honestly, loyalty, justice, and so forth.

Accept what comes up for you at face value. Please note that we're not asking you what's important about life to your parents, your spouse, children, boss, whomever. The most unhappy people we know are those who try to live their lives by someone else's values. The power of this exercise lies in expressing what's true for you, not what you think someone else would want to hear.

Most people end up with eight to twelve items on their list. Don't worry about adding more or having too many; simply continue until you run out of things to add.[2] You can start writing your answers down now.

What's Important About Life to You?

---

[2] Some people are tempted to cut this exercise short. Not you, of course, because you're doing the exercises in the way we suggest. However, there's an interesting story about why shortcuts don't work on page 97.

Once your list feels complete to you, your partner will take the lead. Hand your list over; your partner's instructions follow. If you're both doing the exercises in *Clients Forever*, you should each finish your personal lists before you exchange them.

IT'S A MATTER OF PRIORITY (PARTNER'S INSTRUCTIONS)

Your job is to find out which item on your friend's list is the most important. Please read these directions all the way through before you begin.

You're going to compare each item on the list against the others until you find the one that's more important than anything else. You'll repeat the following six steps until the list on the left is replaced by a new one on the right side of the page.

1. Compare the first and second items on the list. Say something like this:

> You can have everything on your list. You can have it all. But if you had to choose between (first item) and (second item), which would you choose?

2. Wait for the answer. (We know you're not the person who needs us to tell you that. It's the other guy reading *Clients Forever*.)

3. Ask the same question, using the answer your friend just gave and comparing it to the next item on his list.

4. Continue the process, each time keeping the item your friend chooses and comparing it to the next one on the list.

5. When your friend has chosen between the last two items on the list, write the final choice at the top of the right side of the paper, and cross it off the list on the left.

6. Repeat the process with the remaining items on the left-hand list.

An example will help. Let's say your friend has a list like this:

Financial security
Respect
Health
Family
Humor
Free time
Travel

You say, "You can have everything on your list. You can have it all. But, if you had to choose between financial security and respect, which would you choose?"

Your friend chooses respect over financial security.

You then ask, "Which would you choose, respect or health?" Notice that you don't ask what he means by respect or health. You just use the words or phrases your friend wrote down.

He chooses respect again.

"Which would you choose, respect or family?"

This time, he chooses family.

"Family or humor?"

Family.

"Family or free time?"

Your friend might hesitate because he just realized that family and free time overlap. If he had more free time, he'd enjoy his family more and feel more a part of their activities. Yet he thought of them initially as two different things.

Your job is to get him to choose one.

"Remember that you can have it all. For right now, just choose one, please. Family or free time?"

Family.

"Family or travel?"

Family is the answer that remains after you've gone through the list the first time. You cross it off the list on the left and write it at the top of the right-hand column.

Then you start over with the first item on the left hand list. If you crossed it out, begin with the next item.

"If you had to choose only one, would you choose financial security or respect?"

Respect.

"Respect or health?"

Respect.

"Respect or humor?" (You skip family because it was transferred to the other list.)

And so it goes, until you've asked your friend to compare all the items on his first list, one by one, against the others. Each time you get to the bottom of the list on the left, you cross the final preferred item off and transfer it to the right side of the paper. The list of items to compare against each other grows shorter as you move through the process.

At the end, your friend's list might look like this:

Family
Respect
Health
Free time
Financial security
Travel
Humor

Or it might look like this:

Financial security
Free time
Travel
Humor
Health
Family
Respect

There's no right or wrong way for the list to end up. By the way, at some point in the process, you might think your friend forgot to include an important item on his original list: love, friendship, financial security, whatever. He didn't. It's *his* list; not yours.

Feel free to make your own list and to go through the process yourself. You don't have to be a sales professional to benefit from a better understanding of your priorities in life.

WHY SHORTCUTS DON'T WORK

When we do this exercise in workshops, two experiences are consistently true for participants. First, comparing each item against the others is often harder than they expect. Second, they're surprised by what they find out.

These experiences provide evidence that you can't do an end run around the process. By comparing each item against the others, you're more likely to end up with a list that reflects what's *really* important in your life, as opposed to what you *think* is important to you.

Here's what a few workshop participants have to say about the process:

> I just found out that some things are more important to me, particularly one thing that wasn't on the top of my priority list in my mind before I did this. That was major.

> When Bill was doing his list, he mentioned financial security. I looked down at mine, and I realized it wasn't on my list at all. And I went, *whoa*.

> One thing that shocks me is that I put my husband second. My children and then my husband. If you had asked me at 7:30 this morning where my husband fell on that list, I would have said 15 out of 8.

> My financial independence was the last thing on my list. Oddly enough, religion came in third.

Here's a more expanded story about the surprises that await when you go all the way through this process.

We first did this exercise in 1987 with a close business associate. He said, right off the bat, "I'll just tell you, it's financial independence. That's number 1 for me."

"Fine, but let's just go through the process," we said. Lo and behold, integrity came out number 1.

He said, "Well, let's save some time. I know financial independence will be number 2."

Family came out number 2.

He tried one last time, "OK, now I *know* financial independence will be number 3."

We persisted. "Let's just do the exercise."

Financial independence eventually came out number nine for our associate. He was shocked—it seemed to him that most of his efforts in life were geared toward making more money. However, at that point, he was struggling with a huge debt. He didn't have money to pay all his bills and had to figure out how to handle the ones he couldn't. Because he was so aware of his urgent need for money on a daily basis, it was a huge, energy-sucking squid that he believed was most important to him. When he went through the process of weighing each value against the others though, he realized that money was actually at the bottom of his list of priorities.

COME INTO THE KITCHEN FOR A MINUTE

We'll close this chapter by putting your list of priorities into a framework that tells you a little more about them. Draw a horizontal line through your reordered list of values, between items number 3 and 4. Do the same thing between items 6 and 7, and between items 9 and 10, if you have that many. Your list should now be divided into sections consisting of three values each.

Fulfilling the values of your life is much like baking a cake. Think of the top three items on your list as the most basic ingredients needed to bake a cake: flour, some kind of leavening, and liquid. (We know that some of you rely on different ingredients for making a cake: a phone, a car, and a bakery. Just pretend you know how to turn your oven on so you can play along.) With these, you can make many different kinds of cakes. Without them, you'll bake something, but it won't be a cake.

The values that fall in the top third of your life list are the most basic ingredients to a life that works for you. Whatever they are, they're fundamental to your sense that all's right in your world. If these values aren't being fulfilled, then your life just doesn't work.

Now let's say we're not making a dull and boring cake, though. We're making a special cake, one that is uniquely yours. You'd want some flavors in there, like chocolate, cinnamon, applesauce, banana, lemon, vanilla, nuts, allspice, and so forth. You can have whatever kind of cake you want.

Values 4, 5, and 6 on your list are the elements of your life that give it the flavor you really like. They add depth and richness to your experience of being alive.

You've got a delicious cake now, but what about frosting? You could get along without it just fine, but it kind of holds the whole cake experience together. Your seventh, eighth, and ninth values are like frosting.

Everything else on your list is like little candy gizmos. Take them away and you still have a delicious cake. Your life works pretty well without the values that come after number 9, but they're nice to have if everything else is working for you.

The important thing to realize about this example is that the first three items on your priority list drive your life. These items on your list, whatever they are, bake your cake.

You can also look at the order of your priorities and realize if you're likely to experience some conflicts. Let's say, for instance, financial security and health are numbers 1 and 2 on your list. If you have a choice between taking care of yourself—working out or going for a walk—and pushing a little bit harder to add to your financial security, you're more likely to make the extra call or attend the extra meeting because financial security is your top priority.

Or let's say that relationship is number 1 and integrity is

number 2. Would you fudge the truth a little if you thought your relationship was threatened? Possibly.

BACK TO THE SEVENTH GENERATION

If you're like most people who do this exercise, you learned something new about what makes you tick. As we said earlier, the insight you gain makes it worthwhile to go through the process.

One of the benefits of doing this exercise in a workshop setting is being able to see and hear how different people have different priorities. You might think a group of sales professionals sitting in the same room would have pretty similar goals in mind. Over the short term and strictly in terms of their business, group members probably do—get the award, win the trip, set the record. You might expect financial success to show up near the top of almost everyone's list. But, in reality, it's not even close. It's often low on the list or absent.

This prioritization is particularly interesting because many fifth- and sixth-generation sales efforts focus on finances to clinch the sale. Sales professionals pitch a higher return, a lower outlay, or better interest rates. The relatively low value of money in a roomful of people suggests that money-centered pitches miss the mark—big time.

Our larger point, though, is about diversity in general. Over the long run and in terms of who they *really* are, values couldn't be more different from one person to the next. We don't understand what's important to somebody else because we don't take the time to ask the question or to look behind the generalizations.

The same is true for your clients and prospects. It's a mild form of insanity to believe that *you* know what they want. The unrecognized obvious here is that you have no idea how your clients' and prospects' life lists appear. None. We're not suggesting that you elicit it, either. Just know that anything you believe about what's really important to your clients and prospects is probably a misconception.

We hope that another benefit to you of having done this exercise is that you've learned something about validation. If your partner sensitively followed our flawless directions to the letter, you should have experienced an environment in which you felt free to express yourself fully. Ideally, your partner's responses were so accepting that nothing distracted you from discovering new things about yourself.

Think back about what your partner did that helped you focus on your own experience. Perhaps he listened well and didn't sidetrack the conversation in any way. On the other hand, if your partner, say, exclaimed, "Hoo boy!" and rolled his eyes when you handed your list over, you might have felt less than completely willing to be open.

Take a moment now to reflect on what kind of responses from your partner worked for you and what kind you'd like to avoid inflicting on your own clients and prospects. Write them down below. The act of writing brings your reflections into a form that you can focus on, learn from, and refer back to.

RESPONSES THAT WORKED

RESPONSES THAT DIDN'T WORK

Pat yourself on the back. Pat your partner on the back, too. You accomplished quite a bit by doing these exercises. If we were in a workshop, we'd take a few moments to go over everything you discovered about what's important to you, what it was like for you to be honest about your priorities with someone else, how validation helps discoveries happen, or anything else that came up for you.

We can't have that conversation with you. We can, however, recommend that you take a day or two to let the experience sink in. Talk about it with someone other than the individual who helped you with the process. Saying things out loud makes them more real.

Ya'll come back now. We'll leave the light on for you. Things get even more interesting in the next chapter.

CHAPTER 7

So, What Are You Going to Do About It?

Now you know what your true priorities are. However, having knowledge and doing something about it are different things.

Knowledge takes on meaning when you put it into action. That's what this chapter is all about—how to infuse your way of being with a sense of purpose that springs from what's most important to you.

This is another exercise that's great to go through, even if you're just interested in recreational self-improvement. More importantly, though, it's key to being in the world in a way that reflects what you're all about.

Once again, the benefit of this exercise is twofold. In all likelihood, you'll discover some things about yourself that you didn't know before. And, by doing it with another person, you'll learn what it feels like to speak your truth, your whole truth, and nothing but your truth.

PRIOR PRESENCE

Speaking your truth transforms your relationships with clients and prospects. All the exercises in *Clients Forever* are geared toward making that experience easier for you. Each one makes you aware of a different aspect of what's true for you. You also repeatedly experience what it's like to be validated, not violated, for telling someone else about it.

The impact of knowing yourself and showing up in the world fully as who you are extends into circumstances of which you won't even be aware. As the people in your community start to talk about your unique way of doing business, they—even the ones you haven't met—understand something about who you are, as well as what you do. We call this *prior presence*.

A powerful way to establish prior presence is by being willing to show up and put yourself out there, without masks or facades. You're not politicking or positioning or schmoozing. Seventh-generation sales is the opposite of schmoozing. You could think of what you're up to as antischmooze training, in fact.

Here's an example of what we mean. Have you ever been in a business meeting where everyone is talking about doing a particular project in a certain way, and it doesn't feel quite right to you? You feel uneasy, yet you don't want to rock the boat because everyone else, it seems, is with the program.

Out of the blue, somebody says, "Wait a minute. I don't know about the rest of you, but this doesn't feel quite right to me. What do you think about doing this and this and this instead?" She's not manipulating; it's not a power play. It's just what she really thinks and feels, and it rings true for everyone *because it is true*. Her honesty blows through the room like a gust of fresh air. Our workshop participants use words like *hero* and *leader* to describe people who are willing to be completely honest in this way.

We're talking about the same kind of experience, when who you're being consistently rings true for the people around you. Creating a prior presence doesn't take keen strategies. It doesn't require a loud voice, either. Prior presence comes from knowing what you stand for and being willing to speak it clearly. In this chapter, you'll learn more about what you stand for.

AND NOW FOR SOMETHING ENTIRELY DIFFERENT

The process of discovery you're about to experience is so unique that most people have never gone through anything similar. Afterward, you'll understand—more completely than you do now—what the items on your life list mean to you. You'll also get an idea of how they reflect your highest and most important purpose in life.

In this exercise, your partner will prompt you to think more and more deeply about why you value what you do. You won't write anything down; your partner will. Then he or she will look for the pattern that runs through your answers.

Remember that, in the last chapter, we asked you to record your spontaneous answers without dwelling on the words you used. When you did this, you unknowingly used a kind of mental shorthand. Words or phrases substituted for a more developed idea in your mind. You may not even be consciously aware of all that these ideas involve.

In Chapter 2, we explored the difference between generalizing and making distinctions. Remember that generalizing requires less insight and understanding than making distinctions does. When we hear a word like *integrity* or *security*, for instance, we usually assume we know what it means. We mentally step over that word and go on.

In truth, though, the more sophisticated our thinking is about a particular concept, the more we distinguish between various possible meanings. A notion like integrity—or each of the items on *your* life list—has different shadings, depending on whose mind it rests in.

Let's use the example from the last chapter of the business associate we first did this exercise with. You may recall that he expected his highest value to be financial independence, but he discovered that he valued integrity more than anything else.

Our highest value also turned out to be integrity. Now an uneducated thinker (not you, because you know how important distinctions are) would normally generalize and assume that we both had the same top-priority value.

Here's the interesting part: We meant two different things. To our associate, having integrity meant he always kept his word. To us, having integrity means we do what's best for everyone involved in a situation. We had the same label for what was most important to us. What we meant by that label, though, was different, and we behaved according to our implicit meanings, not the label.

In this exercise, you'll look behind the responses—or labels—you gave to the question, *What's important about life to you?* For each subsequent answer you give, you'll look behind that, too.

The rest of this chapter contains the exercise that will help you understand what you mean by the words and phrases you chose in the last chapter. The person who's helping you should definitely read it. You can, too, especially if you're partnering with someone to do the exercises in *Clients Forever* together. The power of the exercise doesn't lie in being surprised by what happens; it arises from making distinctions about something about which you've been, until now, happy to generalize.

FOR THE PERSON DOING THE ASKING (PARTNER'S INSTRUCTIONS)

In this exercise, you'll be helping your friend uncover the meaning behind the answers he or she gave to the question, *What's important about life to you?* The process is simple; the key is listening well and noticing patterns.

Read through the following instructions and example. They're pretty lengthy, so make sure you take time to read them all the way through at least once before you start. After reading them, you may think this is a difficult exercise. It's not. Thousands of workshop participants have learned to do it in a matter of minutes.

As is the case with all the exercises in *Clients Forever*, there are no right or wrong responses. They conform to a three-tiered pattern, though, which works like a roadmap for you during the process. You can tell where you are by the kind of responses you hear.

The first-level answers your friend gives will most likely be about his current situation. As you continue to ask the question we suggest, he'll move into second-level answers, which are generally about making a difference in other people's lives or in the world. One of the hallmarks of third-level responses is a spiritual-sounding concept, like higher self or higher purpose.

Here's how to proceed:

1. Make sure you have your friend's life list in front of you.
2. Get several clean sheets of paper and something to write with. (See how easy this is? You've already done 20 percent of the steps involved.)
3. Choose a single item on your friend's list of priorities. It doesn't matter where you start—top, bottom, or smack dab in the middle. Let's say you choose an item called *health*.

4. Ask your friend what's important about that value. Say something like this: "What's important about health to you?"

5. We won't tell you to wait for the answer. You learned that valuable technique in the last chapter.

6. Write the answer at the *bottom* of the page. Let's say your friend responded, "I feel good, so I have all the energy I need." If your friend rambles so much that you lose the thread of the point he's trying to make, ask him to restate his main point concisely, and write that response down instead.

7. Ask what's important about whatever you just wrote down. You'd say something like this: "What's important about feeling good so that you have all the energy you need?"

8. Record the answer *above* the first one. Yes, you are making a list of long notes that will run from the bottom to the top of the page.

9. Repeat until you get the final answer, which you'll learn to recognize as you read on. Cross-check it (you'll learn how to do this, too).

10. Repeat steps 3 through 9 until a pattern emerges.

An Example

This is a transcript from an actual workshop. We talked with Dave in front of an audience; they participate toward the end of the process. The names have been changed to protect the participants.

CLIENTS FOREVER: We'll start with real estate household.[1] Okay? What's important about real estate household to you?

DAVE: Well, household would be like living in a large, comfortable home. Number one on that list would probably be the

---

[1] "Real estate household" doesn't make much sense when you read it, does it? However, it's the phrase written on this person's life list. This example illustrates that the only person who has to understand the life list is the person to whom it belongs. Enjoy being in the dark.

house we live in, a large, comfortable home with custom fur-
nishings and very comfortable and a safe haven to be.

    CLIENTS FOREVER: Can I abbreviate that to a safe haven?

    DAVE: Okay.

    CLIENTS FOREVER: Is that okay with you?

    DAVE: Yeah, with luxury.

    CLIENTS FOREVER: So, it's a luxurious safe haven.

    DAVE: That will do it.

There may be a few people in the universe who speak in
complete sentences that flow in a logical sequence. Most people, though, use phrases that start and stop in midair, repeat
themselves, say "um" a fair amount, and, in general, muddle
through to their point. Your most important task as a listener is
to ferret out the core of the answer you receive—that's what you
write down on the page in front of you. (In workshops, we write
the responses down on a flipchart. You can use a flipchart, too,
if it'll make you feel more official.)

Notice that we repeated Dave's exact words and then
checked to make sure the abbreviation conveyed the sense he
was after. We wrote down "luxurious safe haven."

Let's continue with the conversation:

    CLIENTS FOREVER: Luxurious safe haven can mean different
things to different people. So, let's look at what's beyond that.
What's important about having that to you?

    DAVE: Well, it gives me a sense of—of a nice lifestyle and a
place to invite friends and family into to entertain and just to
look forward to going—when you go home and it's—it's comfortable and it relaxes you and you're happy.

Dave's answer here is what we'd expect. He just wants to
come home and relax. The first time or two, responses to the
question, *What's important about that to you?*, revolve around

fairly immediate and commonplace concerns. These are first-tier answers:

> CLIENTS FOREVER: So, what's important about having a place that relaxes you where you can be happy? What's important about that to you?
>
> DAVE: Well, it leads to peace of mind, less stress. It's a pride of ownership and, you know, those are things that tie into it, I think.
>
> CLIENTS FOREVER: Okay. Let's put pride in there also. What's important about having this kind of peace of mind to you?
>
> DAVE: Well, peace of mind leads to a—typically a good lifestyle, you know, a relaxed lifestyle. Let me think here a little bit.
>
> CLIENTS FOREVER: It's okay.

Dave's request to think a little bit means that he's running out of material at the first level. It'll get harder and harder for him to continue to answer the question, *What's important about that to you?*, without thinking at a higher level.

> DAVE: And being at peace with oneself certainly and satisfied with what you have done and you're doing with your life is the right thing and you're doing—you're making the right decisions and making good decisions. I don't know that you're making the right decision, but you're making good decisions that will be beneficial to both yourself and your family.
>
> CLIENTS FOREVER: Okay. Can we say making good decisions? Because that provides for your family the way you're talking.
>
> DAVE: Um-hmm.

Dave brought up his family. That's a clue that he's moving to a higher level of thinking, because second-level answers involve a benefit to other people. *Sending my children to college.*

Setting a good example. Being able to provide. Being able to ex-press love. Their lives will be better. Leaving a legacy.

Your friend might move from first- to second-level responses in a single question or several. It doesn't matter how long it takes. When he or she gets there, you know the conversation is on track.

> CLIENTS FOREVER: Let's say you've lived your whole life in this way. You've provided for your family the way you wanted. So you know you've made those good decisions. What's important about having lived a life like that to you?
>
> DAVE: Well, that you'll be remembered as a person who has intelligence, smarts, integrity, and probably gained the respect that you—we would hope to receive from that.
>
> CLIENTS FOREVER: And so what's important to you about having lived your life in such a way that you've gained that respect?
>
> DAVE: Well, fulfillment of your mind, I guess. I mean, sort of these things all sort of run along in my way of thinking, but . . .
>
> CLIENTS FOREVER: I think so too.
>
> DAVE: And feed one another and they feed off one another.
>
> CLIENTS FOREVER: Yeah.

Notice that, as it got harder for Dave to find words to express his thoughts, we were slightly more verbally active. One of your jobs is to help your friend relax and take the time to find the answer. The best way you can help is by being comfortable with the silence, interjecting an occasional monosyllable to let your friend know you're still listening.

The vast majority of people have never been asked to talk about what's important to them in this much detail. They have to search within themselves for the answers to these questions. That's why they have multiple answers at each tier and sound like they're thinking out loud. That's also why this is such a powerful experience—it's totally new territory.

We encouraged Dave without interpreting or adding to his answers. You can do this, too; it will come naturally to you. You might not sound like us, and that's just fine.

> DAVE: Just fulfillment, I guess.
> CLIENTS FOREVER: Personally?
> (Dave nods.)
> CLIENTS FOREVER: Yes. What's important about fulfillment for you?
> DAVE: Well, let me—I'm trying to put the right words into this one.
> CLIENTS FOREVER: Perfect. That's the perfect response.

We weren't kidding. That really was the perfect answer. It let us know that Dave was just about to move into the third— and last—level of response. It can be difficult to put words around what's behind the last few responses. Some people blast through the process with ready answers, but, typically, it's a little challenging:

> DAVE: I'm a little bit mixed on the emotions or where I should go with this. You know, I'm just thinking that—you know, I wasn't put on this planet just to breath air. I had achieved my purpose and I did good will toward men and for myself and other mankind, I guess.

Occasionally, someone wants to bail out of the process about now—or before this point. As the listener, this is a time to be even more encouraging and accepting than you've been up until now. You can let your friend know that you understand it's hard to keep answering the same question.

> CLIENTS FOREVER: I don't want to put on the spot, where you think you're going to give a wrong answer. There's no wrong an-

swer, but if you lived your life in such a way that you know that you did good will toward mankind, what's important about that kind of life to you?

DAVE: That's as close as I can get.

CLIENTS FOREVER: What's as close as you can get?

DAVE: I guess—I don't know. I think it gets back to the self peace, you know, peace of mind. I mean it sort of gets right back into that. When you've done—you have a—you've accomplished goals, you've gained respect, you've done a lot of good deeds for—for people, your family and—and that's important to us.

The ultimate answer—the one that lets you know you're done asking—is in third-level territory. It can also be very hard for people to put into words. Even the most articulate person might hesitate or say, "It's like—it's like—" You, the listener, have to pay close attention.

Typically, there are two parts to third-level answers. Both invoke a larger frame of reference and place an individual's life in a grand scheme, with or without explicitly spiritual or religious language. You'll hear the first part of a third-level answer when your friend talks, in some way, about *doing* what he or she is meant to do: fulfilling a destiny, living a complete life, filling a life purpose, living God's will. Dave said "I wasn't put on this planet just to breath air. I had achieved my purpose."

The very last answer to this series of questions is even higher-level thinking than the last. It's about a state of being: at peace, done, complete, one with the universe. Dave used the word *self-peace* and the phrase *peace of mind to* describe the state of being.

You'll also get the sense that your friend is using unsatisfactory language to describe doing and being. The words don't match what he or she is feeling and trying to express.

You have just one more question left. This is what we referred to as the cross-check in step 9 of the process. You might be glad to hear it's a *different* question.

CLIENTS FOREVER: Is it fair to say that you have a sense of what it's all about, but the English language, as rich as it is, isn't quite accurate enough to label it?

DAVE: Yeah. There's not a vocabulary to put the right word on it.

In our workshops, participants who volunteer to go through this process publically agree, to a person, that the concept they're trying to articulate can't be accurately named.[2] Now, it's possible they're just so darn glad we asked them a different question, they'll agree to anything we suggest. However, the comprehension and relief that flash across their faces make us think that we're offering them something solid.

The final stages contain what are typically very powerful insights. Most people would be content to stop here, feeling like their time had been very well spent. There's more to the process, though, so keep moving along.

Next, you'll repeat everything you just did. You'll replace the sheet of paper you just used with a clean one, and pick another item from your friend's life list. Again, you'll make notes about what you hear, beginning at the bottom of the page and working up.

CLIENTS FOREVER: Let's do integrity. Okay. I'll ask you the same question. What's important about integrity to you?

DAVE: Well, integrity is doing what you say you're going to do. Your word is your bond. In other words, you say I'm going to do this, I'll take care of this for you. If you're doing it, it's done. People are not going to second-guess or second-question you. It's the fact of the matter. He said he's going to do it and it's done.

CLIENTS FOREVER: Okay. Do what you say you'll do. What's important to you about doing what you say you'll do?

---

[2] Let's have a moment of silent appreciation for Dave, who bared his soul to seventy-five people, real-time, and countless thousands in this book.

DAVE: Well, people trust and rely on you.

CLIENTS FOREVER: And what's important about having—

DAVE: When they trust and rely on you, you become bonded or you become friends.

CLIENTS FOREVER: Yes. And what's important to you about being bonded and friends to someone?

DAVE: Well, friends, we build a social atmosphere, which is a healthy environment to be able to be around and communicate with people. So, social circles, I guess.

CLIENTS FOREVER: Okay. What's important about those social circles and a healthy environment that we're talking about to you?

DAVE: Well, social circles can do a couple of things. You can, you know, in a business environment you can use it as a reference source or a lead source certainly.

CLIENTS FOREVER: Yes.

DAVE: You can also use it as a tool just to—for entertainment, peace of mind, you know, people coming over to you and you're happy when you're talking to people. You know, I don't want to be around people twenty-four hours a day, but in my— I can pick and choose, and like most of us probably do, so I mean, we either have friends over to dinner or maybe go to a gathering or whatever, those are all healthy environments for myself.

CLIENTS FOREVER: Okay. So, we're just going to say that you said happy, peace of mind. So, what's important about living your life in such a way where you're happy and you have peace of mind?

DAVE: Look at where we ended last time. It goes the same place.

The process can be quicker the second time through, although some people struggle more than they did the first time. Here's what happened next when we were working with Dave:

CLIENTS FOREVER: All right. So, we could start again. What's important about money to you?

DAVE: It's peace of mind.

CLIENTS FOREVER: What's important about your family to you?

DAVE: Well, use the same phrase all the way through.

Almost everyone starts seeing the pattern hidden behind their values list pretty quickly. That's why it doesn't matter which one you start with; they all end up in the same place.

This insight is uniformly a very surprising and significant one. The original items on the priority list seem to reflect very different aspects of your friend's life. Dave, too, was very surprised to learn that they all ended up at the same place. For him, it was peace of mind. Once a pattern—whatever it is—seems clear to your friend, you don't need to go through any remaining items on the list.

At this point, you know enough to start helping your friend clarify why his values are important to him. You might still feel a little daunted by the process we described. Of course, you can review the directions, if you'd like to. However, most people find that the process becomes quite clear once they start to go through it.

Continue until your friend sees the pattern in his responses.

Looking for the Ultimate Pattern

Seeing the pattern revealed is a significant insight. Many people would be content with knowing why they value the things about life that they do.

However, there's more. The next part of this exercise takes just a few minutes. In it, you have the chance to help your friend discover the purpose of his life. You'll do that by looking for a different common thread in his responses.

You should have a few sheets of paper in front of you. Each one contains a list, written from the bottom to the top of the page, of concise statements your friend made as he searched for the reasons for choosing the items on his life list.

On each of those sheets of paper, focus on the statements

that came later in the conversation, the second- and third-tier responses. Look for common words and phrases. These words—the ones that show up in the second- and third-level responses—are a clue to the core purpose that drives your friend's life. Write them on a separate sheet of paper.

Life purpose is different than an occupational role. You can have the same life purpose and fulfill it in a number of ways. The life of the late Dr. Benjamin Spock provides an example of someone whose life purpose was evident in his many roles.

Remember that Spock was the first expert on child care who advocated respecting children. "They deserve respect," he said, "and they'll grow up to be better people." He wrote the book that became the child-rearing bible of a generation of parents. Later in life, the former political conservative became a vocal opponent of atmospheric nuclear testing and the Vietnam War. "It took me until my sixties to realize that politics was part of pediatrics," he said.

We never had the opportunity to question Dr. Spock about his values and to see what pattern emerged in the words he used. Upon his death, though, his life purpose was described as "improving the lives of children" by President Clinton. While we might choose different words, it seems apparent that a single thread winds through his roles as pediatrician, author, and activist. The point here is the pattern, not the political leanings.

The elements of your friend's life purpose are found in statements in the second and third levels of responses for a good reason. Second-level responses are about other people in your friend's life; third-level responses are about a higher calling. To a person, the workshop participants and coaching clients at Clients Forever recognize they're driven by something outside their personal interests.

When you look at the words and phrases in front of you, a pattern may seem glaringly apparent. Sometimes, it's more subtle. Let's check in with our buddy, Dave, and see what the other workshop participants have to say about an emerging pattern:

CLIENTS FOREVER (to audience): Given what we have so far, what would you say Dave's purpose in life is? What's the pattern here? What's he meant to do that really trips his trigger? What does he create?

AUDIENCE: Personal satisfaction. Peace of mind. Healthy environments.

CLIENTS FOREVER: (to Dave): Yes. Your purpose in life is to create healthy environments. Personal satisfaction and peace of mind come from it. Creating healthy environments is over here as luxurious safe haven. It's over here as a healthy environment. Are you with me? Now, this may not be pure, but it's pretty darn close. The essence, the core, of what drives your life is creating healthy environments for yourself and others.

DAVE: Yes.

Here's another example from another class member in a different workshop.

CLIENTS FOREVER: You mentioned, in all three examples, something about leaving a legacy. How would you phrase that? Leave my kids with a legacy? On a scale of 0 to 100, with 100 being dead-on accurate, how accurate does that purpose sound?

PARTICIPANT: 87.

CLIENTS FOREVER: What would it take to make it a 93?

PARTICIPANT: Leave a legacy behind me for my children and everyone else.

Now you can start looking for the life purpose that's hidden in your friend's responses. If you're on the right track, it will feel very familiar to your friend. Deep down inside, your friend already knows what purpose underlies his life. You won't so much come up with a startling new insight as offer words that confirm a gut feeling your friend has had for a long time.

One person we know views his life purpose as "making spiritual connections." He can see the thread of that purpose in his life as far back as the seventh grade.

> I was the guy that girls came to when they wanted to know if a particular boy liked them. Guys, too. I had no problem going up to a girl I didn't know and saying, "Hey. See that guy over there? He really likes you."
>
> Even in junior high school, my job was to help people make connections.

This man now runs a highly successful dating agency. We're kidding. He's actually a corporate trainer, and, while his role seems to have nothing to do with spirituality, that's the purpose he brings to his dynamic and engaging presentations.

As we did, check to see how accurate your sense of your friend's life purpose feels to him or her and make any needed modifications.

Meaty chapter, this. Thanks for your hard work and your help. The reason people seek out this kind of experience—whether it's with a friend, one-on-one with a coach, or in a workshop setting—is because of the power it provides.

Your friend won't ever think of him- or herself in the same way again. We guarantee it.

CHAPTER **8**

WHAT'S AT THE CORE?

This is a good time to pause and get your bearings. If this were a workshop, we'd schedule a short break to occur at this point. If you just completed the exercises in the last chapter, put *Clients Forever* down and take a break of twenty minutes or so. Go for a short walk, get up and stretch, or have a cup of coffee. How about a quick nap? You can even lie down and close your eyes, instead of taking one of those head-bobbing, I'm-not-really-sleeping workshop naps.

Come back when you're refreshed and ready to move forward. The next item on the agenda is your personal mission statement.

If, like us, you wonder whether the phrase "mission statement" has any life left after a couple of decades of constant use, feel free to substitute another word. What you're going to do next is to hone everything you discovered in the last exercise down into a concise statement of your most important goal.

Besides *goal*, you could also call it your *vocation, lifework, calling,* or *quest.* Use whatever word or phrase energizes you and makes you eager to keep going.

PERSONAL MISSION STATEMENT

In the last exercises, you prioritized your values, explored the reasons they were important to you, and found the primary reason—the one to which all other reasons lead. Perhaps your partner also helped you understand something about your life purpose.

People who attend our workshops or sign up for coaching uniformly find these insights to be very powerful experiences. The following are some transcribed comments from actual participants; their names and/or positions have been altered.

> CFO: You know, I had a very interesting thing happen today. I tried very hard to participate in the discovery process without planning ahead. Even though I knew that this could end up in an emotional place, I didn't want to plan what that might be like. I was actually able to get into it enough so that I felt that feeling. It was amazing, you know, talking with Tom, who I've known for a long time. I actually got choked up. Fortunately, he looked away.
>
> AUDIENCE: (*chuckling*)
>
> CLIENTS FOREVER: All right. How many of you found yourselves getting emotionally involved in your answers? Now, look around the room. This is a hardcore group of cynical financial planners. Right? Insurance people and they're going, *whoa*, I got emotionally moved here. So, who else?
>
> MIKE: I found a sense of real understanding and a feeling of

personal contentment knowing a little bit more about myself. And once I had that knowledge, it was a good feeling and I don't feel ashamed about it. I've sort of accepted who I am with honor.

CLIENTS FOREVER: Good for you.

MIKE: What kind of occurred to me is that—

CLIENTS FOREVER: Go on.

MIKE: I get real busy with life and running things and doing things and what I came to realize is how very important my family is. Sometimes, I seem to be running too fast and don't pay much attention to that. Rather than that being a realization that I'm aware of on a surface level, it was something that I actually felt—

CLIENTS FOREVER: Yes.

MIKE: —and I realized that as we grow older and wiser, eventually that's the only relationship we have left. The relationship with our family, because everything else goes away.

For this participant, realizing the importance of his family relationships was a profound insight. It arose when he prioritized his values; family came out number 1. For him, this insight had more impact than anything else he discovered during the process.

For some people, their life purpose is the most meaningful insight. Others find the most meaning in the metareason—the primary reason all their values are important to them. In our experience, everyone who participates in the Clients Forever exercises with an open mind makes at least one discovery—their number 1 value, life purpose, or the overarching reason behind all their values—that they find completely compelling.

What is it about the last set of exercises that really gripped you, mentally and emotionally? What took you to the place that the first gentleman above describes—where your emotions were front and center?

This is the core of your personal mission statement. In the example, Mike's might be: *My mission is to have good relationships with my family.* In the previous chapter, we followed

Dave through the exercise; his personal mission statement might be: *My mission is to create healthy environments.*

Your personal mission statement is simply a way for you to encapsulate whatever you found most compelling about the last set of exercises. It's a brief way of expressing whatever is most important to you right now. Write it down here in language that feels natural to you.

MY PERSONAL MISSION STATEMENT

MAKING THE MOST IMPORTANT CONNECTION

In our experience leading workshops and coaching individuals, people shift when they connect with what's most important to them. We can see it in their faces and body language and hear a different tone in their voices. They look both more relaxed and more alert. They sound calmer and more confident, because they're focused on what they *know* to be true.

We're limiting the details as we describe how people feel

when they connect with what's really important to them. Our description could never do justice to their experience, so we're not going to try.

Take a few minutes now to reflect on how you felt toward the end of the exercises in the previous chapter, when you realized what was most important to you. Jot down a few words to describe those feelings. Your purpose in writing down the descriptions is to cement your experience in your memory. Attaching specific words to your feelings makes it easier for you to reconnect with that experience.

Use whatever words come to mind. Just complete the following statement as many times and in as many ways as you need to, until you feel complete.

When I'm aware of what's really important to me, I am . . .

If you're like most people who complete the exercises in the last chapter, the space above this sentence has some very positive words in it. Look again at the list; they're all adjectives, with maybe a noun or two thrown in.

There are no verbs, no *doing* words. The words you just wrote down describe your way of *being*.

Now you know what we've been talking about all along.

From the beginning of *Clients Forever*, we've made a distinction between what you do—the words and behaviors you use as you move through your day—and your way of being. As we've said, what you do matters far less than who you're being.

Harry Beckwith, author of the best-selling marketing books *Selling the Invisible* and *The Invisible Touch*, puts it this way: prospects don't buy how good you are at what you do. They buy how good you are at *who you are*.

THE KEY TO EVERYTHING

Imagine that, every time you sit down with a client or prospect, you feel exactly the way you did at the end of the last exercise. Whatever words you used to describe that experience, imagine they are the hallmarks of your business life. Imagine yourself feeling that way every single day. Imagine that when people talk about you—what we called establishing your prior presence—they use words like the ones you just wrote down.

In this imaginary scenario, ask yourself a few questions. How do you think people would respond to you? Would *you* want to do business with someone like you just described? Do you think your clients would leap at the chance to refer their friends, family, and trusted business associates to you?

Now you get it.

This is why we told you to just trust us—why we badgered you to follow the directions and do the exercises. And this is why we've said all along—and we'll continue to say it and show you how—that your clients will build your business for you, giving you a life that you love. You can't understand how your way of being impacts your business life until you have the experience that the last chapter makes available to you.

There's more. Talk about having your cake and eating it, too. Not only do your clients build your business for you, you get to *love* how it feels to be in business. Every interaction you have—on the phone, in person, scheduled, accidental, sustained, or fleeting—with another person is an opportunity to rekindle the powerful feelings you had at the end of the last exercise.

Flip back and take another good look at the list of words you wrote. This is who you *really* are. You bring all the potential and power on that page to your life. Our contribution—a relatively minor one—is to help you clear away misconceptions that have kept you from appreciating your potential and power. You bring everything on that page—and more—to your life every day.

Our job was simple to begin with. It gets even simpler from this point on. We just help you learn how to remember, reconnect, and be in the world as who you really are.

CLARIFY YOUR BELIEFS

To show up in the world as who you really are, your behavior must be consistent with what's most important to you. In the following exercise, you'll explore your unwritten, unstated, and usually unrecognized beliefs about certain kinds of behavior. The format is simple. Your partner will ask you eight questions. You'll give as many answers to each question as you can. Your partner will take notes so you can concentrate on discovering what you believe.

Here's the key to this exercise. Answer from the perspective of someone who has the personal mission statement you identified a few pages ago. The way your partner asks the questions will help you do this.

The questions in this exercise ask you to consider what behaviors are important to someone who has the same personal mission that you do. The first question is this: *What should someone who has that personal mission do?*

An example from a workshop will help make this clearer.

This participant discovered, much to her surprise, that her highest value was good relationships with her family.

CLIENTS FOREVER: Mary, what did you realize when you had the strong feelings you describe?

MARY: Instead of knowing that I want to have a close relationship with my family, it's actually *feeling* it from an emotional level. It's so important to have, not just for now. A close relationship is harder to build later.

CLIENTS FOREVER: Okay. So, what should someone who values a close relationship with her family do? Someone who feels as strongly about it as you do.

MARY: Spend time with them.

CLIENTS FOREVER: And what else should someone like that do?

MARY: They would be emotionally involved with them while they're interacting with them.

CLIENTS FOREVER: And what else should someone like that do?

AUDIENCE: Listen?

MARY: Yeah. Listen. Be there with them.

CLIENTS FOREVER: Now, remember this is for her. You can't answer for her. Right? So, what else should they give you? What should they do?

MARY: Share their joys. Share their pains.

CLIENTS FOREVER: What else should they do?

MARY: Sometimes just be there and not even talk. Sometimes just be in the same room or just be around. Be available.

CLIENTS FOREVER: All right.

MARY: Be available if they want you. You know, not where they can't get close to you because you're off somewhere else.

CLIENTS FOREVER: Right. What else should they do, someone who highly values family? What else should they do? Is that it?

MARY: Yes.

The second question is the flip side of the first one: *What shouldn't someone who has that personal mission do?*

> CLIENTS FOREVER: Okay. So, let's ask you the next question. What shouldn't they do?
>
> MARY: Be distant—physically, mentally, emotionally.
>
> CLIENTS FOREVER: What else shouldn't they do?
>
> MARY: Dictate.
>
> CLIENTS FOREVER: What else shouldn't they do?
>
> MARY: Hurt.
>
> CLIENTS FOREVER: Hurt them?
>
> MARY: Sometimes you shouldn't just carry your baggage into that relationship.
>
> CLIENTS FOREVER: Yes. What else shouldn't they do? Is that it?
>
> MARY: Yes. I'm done.

That's all there is to the first couple of questions. What should someone with your life purpose or value do? What shouldn't he or she do?

The other six questions are very similar. Answering them will help you find out what behaviors you believe are possible, likely, and necessary for someone with your personal mission.

HELPING YOUR FRIEND CLARIFY BELIEFS (PARTNER'S INSTRUCTIONS)

This exercise is simple, compared to the two previous ones. You ask questions and write down the answers until your friend has nothing else to add.

Your friend's personal mission statement is at the core of the questions you ask. Flip back and look it over. Commit it to memory or write it down so that you're sure to remember it.

1. You'll need something to write with.

2. Ask, "What should a person whose mission is to [*insert your friend's statement here*] do?" For instance, in the last chapter, Dave's purpose was to create healthy environments. If you were working with Dave, you could ask, "What should some-one whose mission is to create healthy environments do?" You don't need to adhere rigidly to this wording. Capturing the essence of your friend's statement is more important than using the word *mission*.

Other ways to ask this questions include:

> *What should someone who is focused on achieving something big do?*
> *What should someone who is living life fully do?*
> *What should someone whose number 1 value is integrity do?*

3. Write down your friend's answers, without making any judgmental comments, in the appropriately labeled section. Once again, there are no right or wrong responses. Remember that your goal is to provide a safe environment in which your friend can express his or her deepest beliefs about unwritten, unspoken, and, often, unconscious rules for his or her behavior.

4. Solicit more answers with questions like: *And what else should they do? What else? Anything else?*

5. Continue asking the same question until your friend has no more answers.

6. Repeat the process with the next question: *What shouldn't a person whose mission is to [insert the phrase pertaining to your friend's personal mission here] do?*

7. Repeat steps 3 through 5 with the rest of the questions, moving on only after your friend feels complete with the preceding one. By complete, we mean that he or she has no more answers and is mentally ready to move on.

> *What must [a person like that] do?*
> *What mustn't [a person like that] do?*
> *What can [a person like that] do?*
> *What can't [a person like that] do?*
> *What will [a person like that] do?*
> *What won't [a person like that] do?*

This is a fine time to ask the first question. Finish the whole exercise before turning us back over to your friend so he can read on.

I should . . .

I shouldn't . . .

I must . . .

I mustn't . . .

I can . . .

I can't . . .

I will . . .

I won't . . .

WISH YOU WERE HERE

This is one of our favorite moments in our workshops. Participants recap the beliefs they discovered during the previous exercise. We love seeing other people grasp the simple and profound nature of the Clients Forever approach. They're eager to share their insights, and their enthusiasm is infectious.

Since you're not present at a workshop, we're going to conduct a moment of virtual sharing for your benefit. Picture a fellow participant. Let's call him Jay. (The workshop transcript excerpt is real. The details about Jay—including his name—are not. They're just to help you get in the mood.)

Jay's about forty-five and pretty fit, an outgoing, friendly guy. He's wearing khakis and a yellow cotton pullover sweater. He's been a financial advisor for sixteen years or so. When he stands up to speak, you recognize him because he stood right in front of you in the line for coffee during the last break.

CLIENTS FOREVER: All right. So, what did you come up with? What did you discover in the process? Jay?

JAY: Simply terrific. It's pretty funny that on my *should* list, I have an idea that I've known about for years and taken for granted. But when he asked me a question that I really had to think about, it's what I came up with. I should spend more time with each client. It's absolutely vital. I understand it in a whole different way. On the *shouldn't* side, I shouldn't take others for granted, which I do all the time.

CLIENTS FOREVER: You used to.

JAY: List of musts—I was telling Rick that my wife would love to hear me say this; she's never heard it in the twenty years we've been together. I must communicate effectively at an emotional level, not at a rational level.

CLIENTS FOREVER: That would probably double your business, Jay, and I'm not exaggerating. Did you get that?

AUDIENCE: Yeah.

CLIENTS FOREVER: If we communicate on an emotional level, not a logical level, your sales volume goes up and you don't need more clients or prospects to get there. I'm going to generalize here and say that we avoid communicating on an emotional level because we want to protect ourselves with other people. We don't want to be vulnerable. But that means they aren't going to be vulnerable either.

JAY: Mustn't. I was telling Chuck that I had a real hard time trying to verbalize this one, but this is the way it came out: I mustn't mentally talk while others are actually talking. You see, the problem is that in all the years of training I've had, I was learning constantly to be biased.

CLIENTS FOREVER: Yes.

JAY: So, if somebody else is talking I had to be talking to myself in rebuttal to what they were saying. I never heard what they said. So, my must is that I have to shut off mentally and listen.

CLIENTS FOREVER: Yes.

JAY: I will review this every day for thirty days.

CLIENTS FOREVER: Okay.

JAY: I won't set this aside and forget it. I think that's self-explanatory. Can. The most important key thing for myself.

CLIENTS FOREVER: Yes.

JAY: And can't. I can't change who I am.

CLIENTS FOREVER: Right.

JAY: That's it.

CLIENTS FOREVER: Fair enough. Can we thank Jay, please?

AUDIENCE: (*Applause*).

CLIENTS FOREVER: Anybody else?

Some of the comments in the feedback sessions are about the process in general, not specific answers. These can often provide helpful insights.

PARTICIPANT: Well, kind of a funny thing happened with me. I had to go back to the previous step and take a real hard look at what I said was important to me before I began to do it.

CLIENTS FOREVER: Yes.

PARTICIPANT: And, after doing that, I realized what I should do, shouldn't do, and so forth. I really had to be truthful with myself or otherwise there would have been conflict with what I had said before. So, the process required me to respond with more honesty.

We didn't make any of these comments up, not even the part where Jay started with the words, "Simply terrific." We didn't even embellish anyone's words; these are their real reflections on the process. You can tell because, if we had made it up, it would read like this:

PARTICIPANT: My life will never be the same again. I'm on the Nobel Prize nominating committee and *Clients Forever* is definitely in the running. By the way, that's a good-looking suit you're wearing.

BRINGING IT TO THE STREETS

You now have a list of behaviors you believe you should, must, can, or will engage in—and of behaviors you shouldn't, mustn't, can't, or won't adopt. The next step is easy. You'll convert those beliefs into operating principles.

This step is quite straightforward. You'll just restate your beliefs, combining any that overlap into a single operating principle.

The only additional step that can be necessary is to convert any beliefs that are negatively stated into positive operating principles. For instance, Jay said that he shouldn't take people for granted. That belief could be positively restated as "I appreciate the people in my life."

While we're talking about Jay, let's run through a few more of his beliefs and see how they convert into operating principles.

I should spend more time with each client.

Many beliefs can translate into operating principles in a number of different ways. This statement could mean Jay thinks he should spend an additional amount of time with each client during each appointment. It could mean that he should schedule more appointments with his clients. Or, perhaps Jay thinks he should see clients in social, as well as business, situations.

Let's look at this situation from a deeper level. All three of these statements reflect an underlying belief that Jay should treat his clients in a way that reflects how important they are to him. The deeper belief could then translate into this principle:

People are important to me, and I treat them that way.

Jay's next belief is that he must communicate effectively at an emotional level, not at a rational level. That's pretty straightforward:

I communicate about feelings, as well as thoughts and ideas.

Another negatively stated belief of Jay's comes next:

I mustn't mentally talk while others are actually talking.

It's very similar to the positively stated belief that comes immediately afterward:

I have to shut off mentally and listen.

These two beliefs can combine into a single operating principle that could go like this:

I listen attentively when others are talking.

You get the drift.

Now it's your turn. Go back to the list of beliefs your partner helped you create. Scan it for similar beliefs that can be represented by a single operating principle. Restate any negatively worded beliefs into positive statements.

The following are some operating principles from workshop participants and coaching clients to get your creative juices flowing. We offer these as inspiration, not as a blueprint for your own.

I am true to myself.
I live my beliefs.
I do what I say I'll do.
I treat others with dignity and respect.
I show appreciation and love for life.
I express love.
I generate integrity.
I get to the whole truth and nothing but the truth as quickly as I can.
I am a positive influence in the world.
I make smart choices that allow me to be true to myself.
I dream big.
I believe that anything I dream is possible.
I operate with ruthless compassion.
I remain open-minded in my journey.
I am kind and generous.
I communicate honestly and clearly.
I operate with efficiency.
I finish what I start.

I get things done.
I act with strength and certainty.
I set a good example.
I have a balanced and orderly life.
I make the best and most of things.

If you're like many people, you'll tweak your operating principles a little bit before you're completely satisfied with them.
Use a pencil or work them out on a separate sheet of paper before copying your final version into the space below.

MY OPERATING PRINCIPLES

These principles form the foundation of your new, transformed business life. They're uniquely yours, a powerful expression of who you are at your very best. Good work.

CHAPTER 9

WHAT'S WORTH DOING?

You could post your list of principles in your office and count on them to infuse you with a sense of conviction and commitment. In fact, you might want to do so. However, you need to take another step to get the full benefit of the work you've been doing, to turn inspiration into action. To put your set of principles into full operation, you need to define some specific behaviors that are consistent with them.

TAKING IT TO THE STREETS—PART 2

In the next exercise, you'll take a closer look at each principle and identify one or a few practices that put it in motion. Operating practices are more specific than principles. They're *measurable*, which means that someone watching you could easily
tell whether you were operating by your practices.

Let's look again at the example of our new best friend, Jay.
In the last exercise, we took the liberty of assuming that his principle about spending more time with clients could be stated like
this:

People are important to me, and I treat them that way.

Now Jay needs to know exactly how he's going to do that.
A good way to begin to operationalize principles is to identify
circumstances that might or do get in their way. For instance,
perhaps Jay feels like he doesn't have enough time to connect
with his clients before getting down to business. Possibly he's familiar with the experience of feeling his blood pressure rise in
slow traffic, muttering expletives under his breath while looking for a parking space, and trying to catch his breath, smooth
his hair, and check the contents of his attaché while walking up
to the door.

Based on these three potential barriers to operating by his
stated principle, Jay could decide to schedule more time for each
appointment, leave enough time between appointments to keep
one from running into the next, or, if he travels to meet clients
and prospects, make sure he has more than enough travel time.
Or he could also decide to do all three things. In fact, we'd recommend that he create an operating practice for each problem-
atic situation with which he has experience.

They might look like as follows:

*I schedule enough time for all appointments with clients and
prospects.*

I leave plenty of time between scheduled appointments in my office.

I leave myself enough time to travel to every appointment.

Jay's getting there, but these statements aren't quite specific enough. Words like *enough*, *plenty*, and *adequate* are relative. They only have meaning in a given situation. For example, what constituted plenty of travel time one day could leave Jay sprinting up the stairs, too late to wait for an elevator, the next. In the same vein, enough time for an appointment to do routine business with a long-standing client could be far too little for a prospect.

The pitfall of using relative words in operating practices is that they let you fool yourself as to whether you're behaving in accordance with them. Mentally, *almost enough* is just a hair's breadth away from *enough*—and it's the difference between being fully yourself in business and being almost yourself. It's also the difference between having clients forever and having clients for a while.

So what kind of words could Jay use instead of wimpy relative terms? Specific ones—the more specific, the better. Jay needs to figure out what *ample* time means in each case. Again, his experience will tell him what he needs to know.

Let's go back to the first situation, where Jay feels that connecting with his clients is a luxury he hasn't been able to afford. Assume that Jay's habit has been to schedule appointments in his office at forty-five-minute intervals. In that amount of time, he can get through his agenda—but he panics and looks at his watch if his client pulls out a picture of a new baby. Jay could decide to add another fifteen minutes to all appointments for the express purpose of taking care of his relationships with his clients.

That practice could read as follows:

I schedule sixty-minute appointments with clients.

That leaves Jay's appointments with prospects. By revisting past experiences, he could decide that he'd like to do a better job of creating relationships with prospects and apply the same rule.

So the operating practice that now drives Jay's scheduling is this:

I schedule sixty-minute appointments with clients and prospects.

Now Jay remembers that he has a client or two who cannot stop talking. No matter what the topic, these individuals blab on and on. Even an hour isn't going to be enough for them.

Jay's final operating practice about scheduling is as follows:

I schedule at least sixty-minute appointments with clients and prospects.

Now we're going to apply an Imaginary Observer Test to this operating practice. Remember that one of the first things we told you about operating practices was that they're measurable, meaning that an observer could easily gauge whether you're behaving in accordance with them.

To run this test, we're going to imagine an observer standing in Jay's office. Imogene, our usual observer, is holding a clipboard, a stopwatch, and a pencil. She's wearing rhinestone-studded eyeglasses with a chain, pearls, and a pastel cardigan sweater over her shoulders. Imogene has a beehive hairdo and sensible shoes. A stickler for details, Imogene sees and hears everything that goes on in Jay's office.

Could Imogene easily tell if Jay's holding to this practice? Absolutely. She'd just have to glance through his appointment book. Either the appointments are for at least sixty minutes or they're not.

Jay's done with operating principle number 1. Remember that there are two other elements to the "ample" time principle.

Through a similar process of replacing relative words with specific ones and checking how well the rule applies and to whom, Jay comes up with practices to address these elements.

I leave at least fifteen minutes between scheduled appointments in my office.

I add ten minutes to the amount of travel time I think I'll need to travel to every appointment.

Jay's way of being, as represented by the way he does business, is starting to take shape. Let's turn another one of his operating principles into a set of practices. In our experience, each principle is put fully into motion by between one and three practices.

I listen attentively when others are talking.

In our experience, an operating principle like this comes up quite frequently. Listening well is the right thing to do, no matter what situation you're in—and it's key to the seventh-generation process. These are some potential operating practices that go along with listening attentively:

I listen without interrupting.

I ask for clarification if I don't understand something.

I ignore the phone ringing when I'm listening to someone.

I create an environment that helps me concentrate by shutting the door and facing away from the window.

If I become distracted, I acknowledge it, apologize, and ask the speaker to repeat what I missed.

Now it's your turn again. One by one, convert each one of the operating principles you identified in the last exercise into one to four practices that will put it into operation.

The process may seem somewhat laborious or cumbersome, as we've described it. We've separated it into a number of steps to make the process clearer. In truth, the steps can happen simultaneously or in very quick progression. And, while it may take you a few minutes to get your first practice to the point where it passes the Imaginary Observer Test, you'll quickly pick up speed.

Here, again, are the steps to creating the operating practices that go with your principles. Focus on your principles one at a time. Start this process on a separate sheet of paper, copying your final versions into the space below.

1. For each operating principle, reflect on past or hypothetical situations that represent its *opposite*. If your principle is to show appreciation, for example, under what circumstances have you been least likely to do so? When has someone told you he or she didn't feel appreciated? Perhaps you forgot an important occasion or neglected to convey your appreciation for a job well done.

2. Jot down operating practices that would address these circumstances. For instance:

> *I keep track of important occasions.*
> *I say "thank you" regularly.*

3. Strike through any relative words you've just written. Here are some to watch out for:

> *enough*
> *plenty*
> *adequate*
> *sufficient*
> *important*
> *regular*
> *appropriate*
> *critical*

> *I keep track of ~~important~~ occasions.*
> *I say "thank you" ~~regularly.~~*

4. Figure out what you mean by the relative words and replace them with specific ones. For instance, by *important*, do you mean birthdays, anniversaries, and school programs or the date when your quarterly taxes are due? What does *regularly* mean to you? Once a year? Whenever you feel like it? Every hour?

The following are the same operating practices with the relative words changed to more specific ones.

> *I keep track of occasions that are important to my family.*
>
> *At least once a day, I say "thank you" to someone who's done something for me.*

5. Apply the Imaginary Observer Test. Would Imogene know, simply by what she could see and hear, that you were following this practice? If so, you're done.

6. Repeat the process with each operating principle.

We have two more tips for you.

First, some people are tempted to plug recommendations they've heard elsewhere into their list of practices. This defeats the purpose of what you've been doing, and you can tell by the way it makes you feel.

If you've included someone else's recommendation into your list, it feels like an obligation. The operating practices that emerge from the process we've taken you through feel inspiring and energizing. As you imagine yourself doing them, you feel more and more like the person you described in Chapter 8.

Second, you may end up with some of the very same things on your list that you've been doing—or felt inspired to do—all along. You've just recommitted to their importance in your life.

Go ahead and do this exercise now, then record the final version of your operating practices here. You may also want to make other copies to keep at hand elsewhere.

MY OPERATING PRACTICES

THERE YOU HAVE IT

This is your game plan for showing up in the world as who you really are. As you put each one of these practices into motion, it reflects and reinforces the underlying operating principle, the belief that gave rise to the principle, the personal mission statement behind the belief, and the values from which your personal mission statement arose. It reconnects you with the feelings you had during your most powerful experience of doing the exercises in this book.

The internal consistency between your actions, words, thoughts, and feelings that you experience as a result is both freeing and powerful, and it is the foundation of the seventh-generation approach. When you show up as who you are, with nothing to hide, the power of the universe speaks through your eyes.

CHAPTER 10

WHO'S WORTH BEING AROUND?

For a few chapters, we've focused exclusively on you: what you think, feel, and most deeply desire. If you've followed our directions and done the exercises, this effort has paid off handsomely for you.

You now have a clear idea of who you are at your very best—in life and in business. You know what's important to you, and you have a sense of the deeper purpose behind your daily activities—the big picture of your life. You know how it feels to express yourself in a way that's completely consistent with who you really are.

Your newly acquired perspective is, inherently, a good thing.

You may already recognize the impact it can have on your personal relationships. Frankly, when we said the process would transform your life, we meant more than the part of it that looks like business.

However, your business life is our primary concern. While you could do the exercises for strictly recreational self-improvement purposes and experience huge benefits, you have a larger goal in mind.

Your new perspective is the foundation of the seventh-generation process. As you continue reading *Clients Forever*, you'll understand, more and more fully, how it transforms your business life. In the last third of this book, you'll tie everything together, creating the blueprint for a life that you love, created for you by clients whom you love.

SPEAKING OF CLIENTS...

Now we'll put the spotlight on the other half of your business relationships, your clients. In this chapter, you'll fully flesh out your mental image of your extraordinary clients and what it feels like to work with them.

Doing so is important for a number of reasons. First, it's hard to find anything if you don't know what you're looking for. When you have a clear and specific idea of the type of person who fits your ideal client profile, you'll recognize when he or she appears in the flesh.

Second, you tend to hit what you're looking at. As you identify a set of characteristics that you value about your extraordinary clients and your relationships with them, you're more likely to find them in other people. This tendency hearkens back to the red Mustang syndrome we mentioned earlier; if you like red Mustangs, you'll notice more of them on the road.

The third reason why a clear and specific mental image of your ideal client and your relationship is important is that it serves as a yardstick for any relationship at any point in time. Creating a mental image of your ideal client doesn't eradicate people who don't fit your profile. You'll still have plenty of occasions to contemplate taking on a new client who doesn't quite fit the bill or keeping an old client who's become somewhat of a thorn in your side.

Your mental image of your extraordinary clients helps you make a more conscious decision. You'll know exactly what's missing and can decide to proceed—or not—on the basis of that awareness.

If you're like most of us, you may be tempted to take on a client who isn't quite what you're looking for. Doing so can sometimes mean the difference between meeting your expenses and going into the red. If you make a conscious decision to take on a less-than-ideal client, you can do so without expecting a miraculous transformation. People, after all, don't undergo fundamental changes because you want them to. Having realistic expectations releases you and your client from the pressure to be perfect.

Finally, as your business life is transformed as a result of the Clients Forever process, you'll reach a point where you'll have too many clients or will need to become increasingly discriminating about taking new ones on. You can use your mental image of your extraordinary client as a way of determining whom you *really* want to work with and whom you can refer on with no regrets.

GETTING THE PICTURE

We'll begin by asking you to consider three general characteristics of your extraordinary clients: demographics, psychographics, and economics.

Demographics are the basic qualities and characteristics of your ideal client. They include age, gender, culture, religion, education level, employment, industry, marital status, location, and so on. Demographics usually include income level as well, but we've separated that out into a distinct category. After you consider your extraordinary clients' demographic and psychographic characteristics, you'll have the chance to consider their economic status and behavior in detail.

For now, confine your pondering to the short list we've given you. Does it matter where your ideal clients live? Are you tired of driving beyond a certain distance or do you crave the change of pace of traveling? Do you prefer working with men or women? Is there a certain age range that you most resonate with?

Be careful to distinguish between the demographics of your current clients and those of your extraordinary clients. You can work with exactly the kind of clients you most want to, so don't let your present good get in the way of your potential great.

Perhaps all of these characteristics matter to you; perhaps only one or two do. Jot down the demographics of your extraordinary clients below:

The next category, *psychographics*, consists of your extraordinary client's emotional and behavioral qualities. Just for the record, we use this term far more loosely than you'll probably find elsewhere.

In traditional marketing circles, psychographics include rationales, buying histories, and thought processes behind buying decisions. Examples are clients' interests, previous purchases, similar or related products they've used, the length of time they remained with a particular company in the past, and so on. We're snoring already; are you?

Your extraordinary clients are far more multidimensional than their buying behaviors and emotions; focusing that narrowly does them a disservice. More importantly, you enjoy the relationship for reasons that have nothing to do with buying behaviors. Where, for instance, in the tightly wrapped list above does a great sense of humor fit?

For our purposes, think more broadly about your extraordinary clients' emotional lives and behaviors in their relationship with you. You already started this process in Chapter 1, when we asked you to begin creating a list of your extraordinary clients' characteristics. Turn back to that list and consider the characteristics you listed. Don't list any qualities that pertain to financial behavior here; they'll fit into the next section.

Perhaps your perspective has shifted during the intervening pages. Are there additional qualities that you now realize are important? Are there some characteristics you wrote down before that no longer seem key?

Write your modified list of the psychographic characteristics of your extraordinary clients below:

Your extraordinary clients also have qualities that fall into a third category, *economics*. This term encompasses both demographic and behavioral characteristics.

Economics deserve a category of their own. After all, your extraordinary clients' ability and willingness to pay for your services dictate your financial success and cash flow. They determine whether or not your business survives.

Oddly enough, though, many people think about their clients only in terms of income level, the typical demographic descriptor. The implicit assumptions are that if your clients have a certain income level, they (1) can afford to pay you and (2) will pay you. In truth, neither of these inferences necessarily follow from income level.

While income may determine, to a limited degree, ability to pay, it has almost nothing to do with willingness to pay. Like many other people, we've had the experience of being asked to reduce our fees for individuals whose gross incomes were ample. So, rather than using income level as a proxy indicator for ability and willingness to pay, we're going to ask you to focus on what really matters to you.

Consider your actual or potential extraordinary clients. Do they ask for a reduction in your fees? How long do they hold your invoices or bills before sending a check? Do they pay in full or ask for an installment plan? Do they begrudge you compensation or are they grateful for your help?

How much income does each extraordinary client represent for you? Do you want to have a hundred clients, each of whom is worth $2000 in income to you annually, or would you prefer twenty who are worth $10,000 each? By the way, we strongly suggest that you research the answer to this question, instead of using a ballpark figure. Exactly how much is your average extraordinary (an oxymoron, we know) client worth to you in income?

In the space below, jot down your ideal clients' economic characteristics and behavior. Be bold, asking for nothing less than you deserve.

GETTING THE COMPLETE PICTURE

Demographic, psychographic, and economic characteristics are traits formed by circumstance and history. Your clients bring them to all their relationships, including the ones they have with you.

Extraordinary clients are extraordinary, though, not just because of who they are. They're remarkable because of the relationship between them and you. The fourth, and final, category pertains to the give and take of interacting, to the ebb and flow of your affinity for each other.

The central question here is, How do you feel in the relationship? Just like with the other characteristics, there's no gold standard you can invoke, no right or wrong about how you should feel. It's up to you.

Fortunately, though, you don't have to start from scratch when you consider this question. In Chapter 8, you wrote a description of yourself that began with these words: *When I'm aware of what's really important to me, I am . . .*

Rewrite that description in the space below. This time, though, notice that the header is different. We're saying the same thing we've been saying all along, just using different words to do it. When you're connected with who you really are, you become free to be fully yourself with your clients.

In relationship with my clients, I feel . . .

Earlier in this chapter, we pointed out that your list of extraordinary client characteristics is more of a yardstick than a prescription. It enhances your awareness of who you're looking for and increases the odds that you'll find them. The same is true of relationships.

When you have a clear and specific idea about how your relationships with extraordinary clients feel, you know which individuals *look* like they fit the part of your extraordinary clients and which truly do. It's completely possible—indeed, it happens with some regularity—to size someone up as an ideal client and find out, a few interactions later, that the relationship isn't quite right.

Let's imagine that you wrote down four characteristics just above the last paragraph: confident, calm, empowered, and wise. Now imagine that you're interacting with a client, and one of these qualities is missing. *OK, I feel wise, confident, calm— but not empowered. Or I'm definitely empowered, confident, and wise, but I don't feel calm.*

We're not telling you that you have to cut the cord because that's the case. Feel free to continue in a less-than-ideal relationship. The good news is that now you know what's missing and that you're settling for something less than what you really want to experience.

Sometimes, you can have this experience with a client you really like; he or she just doesn't deliver the whole pizza. Here's how one Clients Forever coaching client describes the situation.

> I really liked working with her. She was interesting, had a great sense of humor, and we had a number of things in common. But when push came to shove, I couldn't depend on her to do what she said she was going to. I kept her as a client for a couple of years and finally referred her on.

In our experience, client relationships that start out limping eventually grind to a halt. And, in our experience, of the four categories of client characteristics, how the relationship feels is second only in importance to whether or not our bills get paid in full on time.

Relationships that work are the foundation of a business life that you love, built for you by the very people whose company you relish. While we haven't felt moved to do so in many pages, we feel strongly enough about this point to offer the following dictum.

CLIENTS FOREVER Wise Dictum Number 9
If the relationship works, the details don't matter.
If the relationship doesn't work, the details won't
help.

CHAPTER 11

IT TAKES TWO TO TANGO

So far, we've talked about how your extraordinary client relationships feel to *you*. However, relationships require two people. And you can't create relationships according to a unilateral set of rules. What works for you might not work for your clients.

A relationship that looks, sounds, and feels like a sure thing to you can simply fail to gain momentum. You feel great about who you're being, and your client's demographics, psychographics, and economics line up perfectly. For some reason, though, the two of you never click.

Similarly, a relationship that starts out great for the two of you can sour. Things happen. Even the sunniest long-standing

friendship or marriage is occasionally rocked by misunderstandings and unmet expectations. The same can be true of long-
term relationships with your extraordinary clients.

WHAT TO DO WHEN THINGS GO WRONG

In your personal relationships, you probably have some
ideas about how to find out what's gone wrong so you can focus on fixing it. Perhaps you and your friend or spouse sit down
for a series of heart-to-heart conversations. Possibly, talking
does the trick. If all else fails, the two of you can see a counselor.

Don't worry. We're not going to suggest that you engage in
soul-seaching conversations with your extraordinary clients. It's
a ludicrous notion: *We need to talk about where this relationship is heading* or *I think we should do business with other people, but I'd still like to be your friend.* Obviously, seeing a counselor together is just as silly an approach.

However, you need to know that your clients feel good when
they're doing business with you. Remember that *if the relationship works, the details don't matter.* While we originally stated
this dictum as true for you, it's equally critical for your clients.
Clients and prospects alike stay in relationships that feel good
to them and they get out of those that don't.

What do we mean by "feeling good"? That's a little hard to
say. You know what your yardstick for the relationship looks
like; you've gone through the process of explicitly identifying
what feeling good means to you. In the example from the last
chapter, it meant feeling confident, empowered, wise, and calm.

In all likelihood, your clients won't have a similar list from
which to consciously draw. However, you can be certain that
they have an implicit, even subconscious, list of criteria for relationships. And there's no way that you can know what's important to them without going through a process to elicit it.

You *could* elicit your clients' lists, but, if you'll recall, you went through a long process to create your own. Your list came at the end of identifying what's important to you and prioritizing your values. It would be impractical for you to repeat the whole thing with your clients—and they might find it a little bewildering.

You already know something about what your extraordinary clients *don't* like experiencing in their relationships with you. We've mentioned feeling manipulated, closed on, patronized, and disrespected, to name just four. You knew this intuitively, anyway. Until now, though, you might have relied on pretty gross—as opposed to subtle—signals that a client relationship wasn't working: your phone calls don't get returned, your client starts behaving evasively in other ways, or you find out that person is doing business with someone else.

Using these signals to size up your relationship with your extraordinary clients is a bit like using divorce papers to evaluate your marriage: *Hmmm, haven't gotten them yet, so things must be going pretty well.* (A sensitive aside: We know that the sudden demise of a marriage can sometimes involve a huge element of surprise for one of the partners.)

You need another way to gauge how your clients are experiencing their relationships with you. It's a tool you already possess, too, but it rarely gets mentioned in a business context.

GO WITH YOUR GUT

We're talking about intuition.

We don't mean mind reading or crystal ball revelations. We're referring to the very common experience of sensing that something is true about a person or a situation. Intuitive awareness is gut-level information that bypasses the logical, reasoning part of your brain.

Perhaps you've had the experience of being aware that a deal was going sour or, conversely, that you were absolutely going to turn a certain prospect into a client. Maybe you've had the experience of thinking about someone and answering the phone only to find that person on the other end of the line.

Intuitive awareness generally doesn't shake you by the shoulders and yell in your ear. It nudges you and speaks softly. Although "women's intuition" is an age-worn expression, intuition itself isn't distributed along gender lines. Men have it, too, but they tend to call it by different names. They might "have a hunch" or "just know." At this point, some people think: *Not me. Everyone else in the world may have intuitive flashes, but I don't.* Oh, yes, you do; however, you may disregard them or second-guess them out of existence. Intuition is like the power of speech; you got your fair share, just like the rest of us human beings.

Intuition is an altogether different process than conscious thought. You can't add up objective data to reach an intuitive conclusion.

Intuition is like electricity arcing from one point to another, from one awareness to another. If you hold insulating material up in the middle of the arc, the flow of electricity collapses. Logic is like insulating material to the flashes of intuitive insight. The moment you engage it, trying to reason with or against your intuition, you turn down the voltage of the insight.

For fascinating reading on the topic of intuition, try *The Gift of Fear: Survival Signals that Protect Us from Violence*, by Gavin DeBecker. He describes intuition like this:

> What [people] want to dismiss as a coincidence or a gut feeling is in fact a cognitive process, faster than we recognize and far different from the familar step-by-step thinking we rely on so willingly. We think conscious thought is somehow better, when in fact, intuition is soaring flight compared to the plodding of logic. . . . Intuition is the journey from A to Z without stopping at any other letter along the way. It is knowing without knowing why.

Intuition is the most powerful tool you have for gauging how your clients *feel* in their relationship with you. If you're like most people, you haven't used it much before now; in fact, you were taught to disregard it.

Think before you talk. Everybody who's heard that rule from a parent or teacher, please raise your hand. Now look around the room. Everyone we asked has his or her hand up.

Preparation is the kiss of death for intuition. By the time you prepare a speech, you're no longer referencing your insight. And, on the subject of speaking, any scripts you might use with clients and prospects completely squelch even the *possibility* of insight. Intuition requires that you focus on the present moment in the conversations you have with clients and prospects. If you're thinking about what you said, what you forgot to say, or what you're going to say next, you're not focusing on the present moment.

Using your intuition also requires that you pay attention to your client or prospect's experience, not yours. This requirement should come as no surprise. All along, we've maintained that the key to revelational buying is being so yourself that you can concentrate completely on your clients and prospects.

If you're watching your client for body language you can mirror, you're not seeing what's really going on for him or her. If you're listening for objections so that you can overcome them, you're not hearing what he or she is really saying. Using your intuition requires you to be quietly alert and focused on the other person. Then, just by sitting with him or her, you'll know something about what that person is experiencing.

Think about that statement. Perhaps you've been in the situation of sitting in a public place, in close proximity to a stranger. He doesn't say a word, but you get a sense of his state of mind. You just know somehow that he's upset or completely at peace. You don't do anything about your insight, and you forget it within seconds. However, that's intuition.

We're suggesting that you simply pay attention to gut reactions like these and check them out—not with strangers at a train station necessarily, although don't let us stop you from emulating Mother Teresa if that's your life purpose.

By all means, though, check out your gut reactions with your clients.

HOW IT WORKS

Follow up on your flashes.

That's it. That's the only rule for intuition.

Let's see how it works.

The following are just a few insights you might have during the course of a business week:

I'm late. He might think his business is unimportant to me.
She seems really busy. Maybe she'd like to reschedule.
I'm not the right person to be working with him.
She's distracted by something.
I wonder how Bob [a client] is doing?

The reasoning part of your brain might add to your flashes of insight to keep you from acting on them.

I was late. He might think his business is unimportant to me. . . . But it's too late to go back and apologize.

She seems really busy. Maybe she'd like to reschedule. . . . But I've waited weeks to get in to see her.

I'm not the right person to be working with him. . . . But I really need the money.

She's distracted by something. . . . But I don't know what to do about it. I'll just keep talking.

I wonder how Bob is doing? . . . But I don't have any business to call him about, so it'll seem as if I don't have anything better to do if I call just to talk.

See how your brain "buts" into your intuition's business? Now what would happen if you didn't listen to it?

I was late. He might think his business is unimportant to me. . . . But it's too late to go back and apologize.
I'm going to do it, anyway.
"I'm sorry to stop our conversation, but I really have to acknowledge the fact that I was late. Meeting with you is important to me, and I'm sorry that I kept you waiting."

She seems really busy. Maybe she'd like to reschedule. . . . But I've waited weeks to get in to see her.
I'd rather come back when she can focus on what we need to do.
"I can't help noticing how full your plate seems right now. Would it be better for you if we rescheduled?"

I'm not the right person to be working with him. . . . But I really need the money.
It's not fair to either one of us if I don't say something about it.
"I'm not sure I'm the right person to work with you. I may not have the products [or perspective or background or experience] to give you what you need. Can we talk about that?"

She's distracted by something. . . . But I don't know what to do about it, so I'll just keep talking.
If I just keep going, I'm wasting her time and mine.
"Are you okay? My sense is that there's something going on for you that's upsetting or really needing your attention right now. What's going on?"

I wonder how Bob is doing? . . . But I don't have any business to call him about, so it'll seem as if I don't have anything better to do if I call him just to talk.

*I don't have to stay on the phone very long, and I really am
wondering how he's doing.*

"Hi, Bob. I was just thinking about you. I'm not calling
about anything related to business; I'm wondering how things
are going for you."

Notice that we're suggesting you confirm your intuition with
clarifying questions. Otherwise, you're making an assumption
based on your intuition—and we all know the old saying about
what happens when you assume.

You can be sure, though, that we're not offering these examples as scripts for you to follow. Our only point is to demonstrate how, after an insight arises, your brain tends to immediately "but" in with a reason you should disregard it. Following
up on your flashes is a matter of saying to your brain, in effect,
"Well, thanks very much for sharing. As I was saying . . ."

Then you use whatever words come naturally. You don't
script it in advance. When you're being your most authentic self,
your words will be perfect. And if you're going to broach an
uncomfortable topic, admit that you're not quite sure what to
say. Every time you speak your truth, you engage more and more
fully with your most empowered way of being.

WHAT HAPPENS IF YOU DON'T

Once you start paying attention to your flashes of insight,
you'll find that you want to follow them *because they won't go
away until you do.*

Let's go back to the first example.

*I was late. He might think his business is unimportant to
me. . . . But it's too late to go back and apologize.*

You stifle the impulse to apologize and continue with the conversation. Is that where it ends? No way. You can't forget altogether about being late.

You continue to be aware of your unacknowledged lateness, only it's even harder to consider stopping the conversation now that your first impulse—and more time—has passed. For a few minutes, you halfheartedly listen for pauses into which you could interject an apology, instead of being fully focused on what your client is saying. You gradually become more present until, twenty minutes later, he glances at his watch. You may think *He's still aware that I was late*, even though you have no idea what he's really thinking. While you shake hands at the end of your meeting, you might scan your client or prospect's eyes for reproach.

Let's say this client or prospect eventually declines to do business with you. A part of you wonders how things would have turned out if you had stopped the conversation and apologized. Because you didn't act on your insight, it lives forever, a more or less active thorn in your side.

We call these unfulfilled intuitive flashes *incompletes*. They hang on, unresolved, and keep you from being fully present with your clients and prospects. They take on a life of their own. It's almost as if they're a third person in the conversation who just keeps saying "Hey! Pay attention to me!"

For a moment, turn back to the list of qualities that you wrote in Chapter 8. Does *thinking about something I should have said* fit on that list? Of course not. It's impossible for you to both have incompletes and be who you are at your best.

Your clients know something's up when you have an incomplete because you're not really listening. You're only going through the motions. They can sense your absence and don't understand it. When you address the incomplete, you relieve a sense of confusion on their part and give them permission to be equally authentic with you.

You can see it coming, can't you?

🌿

CLIENTS FOREVER Wise Dictum Number 10
Follow up on your flashes.

🌿

COMPLETING THE SUBJECT OF INCOMPLETES

Incompletes get in the way of your relationships with your clients and others. They also live forever.

Clearly, this is not good news.

You—and all of us—accumulate incompletes. Not only that, but they're like dog doo on the bottom of a slick-soled shoe. They end up everywhere.

Go back to the example of being late to meet with a client. Are you thinking that the only time the incident will bother you is when you're interacting with the particular client? Not a chance.

Let's say you meet someone who knows your client, an individual your client could have referred to you but didn't. You don't know why your client didn't make the referral, but somewhere in the back of your mind, you recall, once again, your failure to acknowledge being late. While you realize that it's not likely to be the sole reason you didn't get a referral, you assume it factors in somehow.

In short, your incomplete ends up contaminating every situation that connects—in your mind or in reality—to the one in which you created it. We're just talking about being late here, so it may not be a huge deal. (Can you tell we live on the West Coast? We set our watches forward a few minutes when we're on business out East.) However, imagine the influence of all the incompletes you're toting around right now. You may not be aware of it, but it's there.

Some incompletes arise from things you didn't say, as in the above example. Others result from things you *did* say, and still others from things you did or didn't do. Some incompletes that you're carrying are of recent origin, and others are years old.

A powerful exercise—and one that's critical if you want to be fully yourself as much of the time as humanly possible—is to clean up your incompletes. Start by thinking about situations in which you said something you wish you could retract or rephrase. Also consider situations in which you held back and now wish you'd spoken up.

Consider both your business and your personal life, focusing on your relationships with siblings, partners, parents, children, and so forth.

In the space below, list the incompletes about things you said that you now wish you hadn't: jokes that offended, thoughtless words that you regret, accusations, and the like. If you're like us, you might also need a separate sheet of paper to record your list of incompletes.

Now consider times when you wish you had said something but didn't—the moments when something was on the tip of your tongue but the conversation moved on before you got it out. Are there people you haven't acknowledged as much as you'd like? Are there people whose importance in your life you don't communicate regularly—or at all—to them? For many of us, incompletes arise from unexpressed appreciation.

In the space below, list the items in this category:

Next, consider situations in which you *did* something you now wish you hadn't. Indiscretions, actions that were beneath you, instances where you caused injury or pain to someone else, youthful experiments that backfired. You'll know what these are—they'll come quickly to mind, just like they have for all the intervening years. List these incompletes in the space below.

Getting the picture of how incompletes impact your life? Let's keep going. Now think of all the times you've held back from doing something that you now wish you had done. As a minor example, consider projects you've started but not finished. Distinguish between projects you've thought about starting and those you've taken action on and then let slide. The first type are just ideas—*seeing the aurora borealis, building a boat, writing a book*. These aren't really incompletes unless these items are things you know you need or truly want to do. Abandoned projects are, however, actual incompletes.

List these types of incompletes in the space below.

There's one last part to listing your incompletes, and it requires you to be scrupulously honest with yourself. Consider if there are people you've hurt, damaged, or offended in some way whose names don't appear on the previous lists. It doesn't matter if you've been hurt in return. Your only concern here is your own actions, things you said and did (or didn't say and do) that caused pain or loss to someone else, whether or not they were aware of it. Write their names in the space below. Sometimes, you'll be aware of having hurt someone without knowing his or her name. In that case, write down whatever words you use as a mental reference for that individual.

NICE LIST . . . NOW WHAT?

Now comes the good part. You get to *do* something about these incompletes. Start by flipping back to the list of characteristics that describe you in your most powerful and best way of being in Chapter 8. Proceed after you've refreshed your memory about how you feel when those qualities are alive in you.

Now consider each item you've written down. If you're like most of us, nothing—said or unsaid, done or undone—on those lists fits with your experience of who you are at your best. Clearly, unless your list of characteristics includes *wanton and selfish* or *oblivious to my effects on other people,* the list of people you've injured is inconsistent with your best self.

Incompletes trip you up in two ways. The first way, as we've mentioned, is that they get in the way of your relationships with clients and others. The second way that incompletes hold you back is that they *get in the way of your relationship with yourself.* Until you finish your incompletes, your best way of being will include a small voice murmuring, *Yeah, but remember when you . . . ?*

So consider your lists. Pick an incomplete, any incomplete, and decide what you're going to do about it. Even though you'll want to take care of all the incompletes you listed, you have to do so one at a time.

There's no right or wrong way to address an incomplete. Trust your instincts. The same little voice that tells you something is incomplete will also lead you to the best way to take care of it.

You can quickly and simply address some of them. If you're aware of someone you haven't appreciated, write that person a letter. If your house or car needs to be cleaned, just do it. If you need to pay bills or balance your checkbook, do it. You don't have to decide to turn over a new leaf here and become a perfect housekeeper or a financial wizard. You're just taking care of things that are unfinished in your life *right now.*

If you have unfinished projects, decide if you want to finish them or acknowledge to yourself that you won't. If you want to finish them, just make a short plan of action and put it in motion. If you decide against completing a project, dismantle it in some way so that you know that proceeding is absolutely out of the question.

Obviously, it's more challenging to address wounds that you've created for other people. You need humility, tenacity, and courage.

Invariably, when we get to this section on incompletes in our workshops, a few people look like deer caught in headlights. From our experience with individual coaching clients, we can surmise that these people have just been busted, as it were, for extramarital affairs or other actions they regret. For instance, we once heard from a registered investment advisor that, for the seven years he'd been in business, he'd lied to his wife about his income. He led her to believe he made substantially more money than he did—and that he'd invested it at rates of return above what he'd actually realized. This process of listing the things in his life that were incomplete—and a whole lot of soul searching—eventually led to his decision to come clean with her.

It was a tough decision to make. He knew his wife might leave him after he told her the truth. However, part of his reason for doing so was that he'd realized he didn't have a real relationship with her, anyway. Because of the enormous, constantly looming incomplete, he wasn't fully present to his marriage. By erecting a facade to protect himself from her disappointment, he had isolated himself.

This experience is true for all of us. When we protect ourselves by erecting barriers to keep others from knowing what we really think and feel, we actually isolate ourselves. We keep others on the far side of a wall—and stare, day after day, at the bricks in front of our own faces. *The truth shall set you free* is not just a religious statement. Until we're willing to speak our truth and accept the consequences, we're trapped behind the false front we've created.

In the situation with the investment advisor, his wife, of course, had noticed that there was something wrong in their marriage. She didn't know why he wasn't available to her emotionally, so her imagination ran wild. She wondered if he was seeing someone else, if he'd done something illegal, if he had fallen out of love with her. They had even sought counseling to deal with their relationship problems.

Of course, the problem wasn't their relationship. It was his lack of honesty about how much money they had and what he was doing with it. His confession relieved him of a huge burden and offered her an explanation for something that troubled her about their marriage. They stayed together, but they could just as easily have decided to divorce. We're not making the point here that finishing your incompletes is a magical spell to fix whatever is wrong with your life. The key thing to remember is that you can't hide your incompletes from other people. They'll know something's wrong, even though they might not know what it is.

You may have to track people down to finish unresolved situations. In the story below, one coaching client we'll call George did.

When I was about fourteen, my best friend said, "George, I found something really neat to do. I've been shoplifting." I said, "Why would you do that?" He said, "It's fun. You never know if you're going to get caught or not." I said I'd try it. That's how I started shoplifting.

I was good. I was really good. The local dime store printed the names of shoplifters they caught in the local newspaper. My name never appeared. I stole a knife off the counter display while the owner was standing behind the cash register right next to me. Pulled it out, got it in my pocket, walked out free. And every time I looked at that knife, it reminded me that I was a thief.

Recently, and I'm over fifty now, I wrote out a list of people I'd stolen from. There were nine, plus one guy whose truck I wrecked and lied about it. And so I had a list of ten people.

I didn't know where these people lived. I didn't know what their addresses were. I didn't even know if they were alive. I started making phone calls. I called people I knew who still lived in a certain area. I'd ask, "Well, you know the person that used to own Central City Grocery in Peoria? What was his name?" They gave me the guy's name and address. That type of thing.

And I wrote letters to every one of them. I told them what had happened, and I sent them a check with the magic of compounded interest included. There was one woman—it took at least nine people and about fifteen phone calls to find her.

I called her by name. I said, "Mrs. Martin?" And she said, "Yes."

"You don't know me," I said, "but my name is George Benowitz. In 1964, did you own a stationary store?"

She said, "Yes, I did. My husband and I owned that."

"Well, ma'am, I have a check here for you." I wanted to start with the good news.

"Whatever for?" she asked.

And then I had to give her the bad news. "When I was fourteen years old, my best friend and I were in the habit of shoplifting, and we stole some things from you. I've never felt good about that."

She said, "Son, I know exactly what you're going to say and I want you to know that I forgive you."

She didn't care about the money, even after I explained how much it was. She said, "You know, when I was twelve, a friend of mine and I went in to Newberry's Department Store. I stole lipstick. I just couldn't live with myself, so I went and gave it back to him and paid for it."

The last thing she said was, "I want you to know how much I appreciate what you've done."

Sometimes, you don't even need to know you've made the connection to complete something that's been hanging. Another client told us this story:

I once had a good friend with whom I had a terrible falling out. We were very close for a couple of years, then I did something that offended her. We stopped talking. She literally wouldn't answer the phone, so we never resolved the issue.

I was very hurt and angry for a long time. I tried all kinds of ways to deal with my feelings. I used to paint as a hobby, so I tried to paint a picture of my anger. That didn't work—it was eating me up, my hurt at how she wouldn't even talk to me so we could resolve things.

Finally, I wrote a short story about it. I'd written poetry as a teen and, when I was teaching college, I'd published academic papers. That short story, though, was the first time I wrote creatively for more than thirty years.

My writing just mushroomed from that point on. I won an award and started getting inquiries from people who wanted me to help them create marketing materials. I loved it, and I quit my job to do it full time.

I realized that my falling out with my friend had indirectly propelled me into a new career that I absolutely loved. From that point on, I just felt grateful to her. But she still wouldn't talk to me, so I couldn't express my gratitude.

I tried writing letters, but I never sent them. I was pretty sure that she wouldn't open a letter if she knew it was from me. A couple more years went by, and I wasn't even sure where she lived anymore.

One day, though, I just had to take care of it. On the Internet, I tracked down the most recent address for her I could find. It was only about six months old, so I figured mail would get forwarded to her, even if she'd moved. I folded a fifty-dollar bill in a beautiful piece of heavy white paper and put it in a similar envelope, with no return address. Then I mailed it from another city, so she couldn't know it was from me.

I sent money because, when we were friends, she was really cash poor. Fifty extra bucks would have made a huge difference in her life. It was my way of saying "Thank you."

I don't know if she ever got the money. I want to believe she did. At any rate, when I put that envelope in the mail, I did what I had to do.

Finishing your incompletes feels great. You have more energy and more focus as a result of taking care of unresolved situations that have been weighing you down. If you're like most people, once you have the experience of addressing one incomplete, you want to address them all.

Even after you get through the lists you made in this chapter, you might find that you keep creating incompletes. Why? You're human. You might still say and do things that you wish you hadn't—or hold back from saying and doing things you know you should.

Now, though, if you've taken our advice and finished some incompletes, you know how radically different you feel when you do. You'll be highly motivated to take care of anything you leave hanging, and we predict that you'll do so more and more quickly. Now, instead of waiting years to tell the truth, apologize, or appreciate someone, you'll do it within minutes.

BUT WHAT DOES THIS HAVE TO DO WITH REVELATIONAL BUYING?

Your intuition—your tool for gauging how your clients and prospects are experiencing their relationships with you—will be clear of the mental and emotional debris from unresolved situations. You can see present circumstances more clearly. You'll be able to pay more attention to the little voice that says, *Hey, I think something's going on here.* The right words to check out your perception will be there when you need them.

All along, we've said that trusting yourself is the key to revelational buying. Trusting your intuition is the key to trusting yourself. If you don't allow yourself to exercise your intuitive capabilities, you can't fully trust yourself. The process of addressing your incompletes lets you know what it feels like when you act on an intuitive impulse. *I should apologize. I have to tell the truth here. I don't want to finish that project. She needs to know how much I appreciate her.*

Acting on your intuition is the best way to both understand how it works for you and strengthen it. Following up on your flashes means that you move, with words or actions, in the direction they lead you. Your intuitive flashes are like muscles; the more weight you give them, the stronger they get.

Your flashes are also like muscles in the sense that you don't start off doing biceps curls with eighty-pound weights. You start small. Follow up on your incompletes the way that your little voice leads you. Try following up on an intuitive awareness in a nonbusiness relationship. Test your strength, play with it, check out your perceptions.

You won't always be right. Even after you've discharged the ballast of your incompletes, your personal viewpoint will occasionally cloud your vision of the present circumstance. That's one reason why we suggest always checking out intuitive perceptions.

As you exercise this capacity, it gets stronger. The stronger your intuition gets, the easier it is to trust it. The easier it is to trust your intuition, the more you trust yourself in every situation.

CHAPTER 12

SEVENTH-
GENERATION SALES

At long last, we're ready to return to the topic of *selling*. We haven't used the *S* word since Chapter 4. Why are we ready now?

Because you are.

You had to go through the previous eleven chapters to understand fully that seventh-generation sales is about who you're *being*, not what you're *doing*. Shortly, we'll explore the questions that demonstrate the seventh-generation approach. Only now could you ask those questions in a way that's totally focused on your client or prospect's experience.

Of course, you could ask these same questions if you had

started reading *Clients Forever* at this point, meaning you had—heaven forbid—skipped all the exercises. The difference would be, though, that you would probably be doing it just to make a sale. Your unspoken agenda would be front and center and, as you learned in the last chapter, your agenda would prevent you from being fully present in the conversation with your client or prospect.

Of course, if it's the right thing to do, you want to make the sale, too. But now you know that there are a few—if not many—things about life that are more important to you than making this particular sale. You know what your life purpose is and how this sale relates to it. You identified the principles and practices by which you operate.

You learned how important it is to validate someone else's experience by listening closely. You had the chance to experience validation, firsthand. Perhaps you even practiced it by doing the exercises in turns with a partner.

You know exactly who you want to be working with and how that relationship feels to you. You know how to gauge whether or not the relationship is working for your client, too. You know to pay attention to your insights about your client or prospect and to confirm them by asking clarifying questions. You know that your gut is a good guide; trust it, and you'll know what to say. You know how to invite logic to step outside for a moment while you talk to your client.

Now, and only now, we can talk about how all this fits with the *S* word.

A LITTLE REVIEW

There's been a lot of water under the bridge since the last time we talked about what the seventh-generation approach is—and how it represents a paradigm shift in seller-buyer relations. If you'll recall, we also used another term to describe seventh-generation sales: revelational buying. This term keeps the focus squarely on your client or prospect—where it belongs. It encapsulates the idea that your client or prospect will make a decision to buy if he or she experiences a revelation.

When your client or prospect experiences a revelation, that person makes a new connection between a current situation, a different, more desirable state of affairs, and a product or service. Remember that people buy for their own reasons, not the ones that you imagine motivate them; whether or not you understand the connection that your client makes is completely irrelevant.

Prospects buy for their reasons, not yours.

Revelations stop when presentations start.

The more you focus on your prospect's revelation, the more likely you are to meet your needs and goals.

Trust.

In Chapter 3, we told you what your only role is: to create an environment in which your client or prospect can experience a revelation. Everything between that chapter and this—all the exercises, in particular—*help you to get yourself out of the way* so your client or prospect can experience a revelation.

All you have to do is gently get the ball rolling.

THE FIRST STEP

An appointment has been made—either by you or your client or prospect. One of you has called the other and arranged a time and a place to meet. You and your client or prospect exchange greetings and pleasantries just like you would in any of the preceding sales generations. In all likelihood, though, because you're now living by your operating principles and practices, even the initial minutes of your appointment feel different to you than they did before you read *Clients Forever*.

The two of you settle in and The Pause happens, the break in your conversation that means, *We're here for a purpose, so let's get to it.* This is the point where, before reading this book, you might have launched into a presentation or asked probing questions about your client's needs. Now you know how those options disserve your client, but what do you do next?

Or perhaps your client or prospect launches into a presentation about the purpose of your meeting, outlining his or her needs, preferences, and requirements. Eventually, though, he or she will pause. How do you respond?

You ask one question. Introduce it briefly, if it seems appropriate, then ask something like this:

If you could develop your _____ in any area whatsoever, what area would you pick?

What goes in the blank? A word or phrase that is most applicable to the reason that you're meeting with the individual. If you were a business coach, you could ask "If you could develop your business in any area whatsoever, what area would you pick?"

If you were a marketing consultant, you might inquire, "If you could develop your marketing in any area whatsoever, what area would you pick?"

A financial advisor: "If you could develop your financial health in any area whatsoever, what area would you pick?"

An information technology expert: "If you could develop your IT in any area whatsoever, what area would you pick?"

A college recruiter: "If you could major in any subject whatsover, what subject would you pick?"

In most of these examples, we use the word *develop*. We like it because it stands in for a whole cadre of related terms: *expand, cultivate, deepen, enrich, evolve, amplify*, and so forth. Depending on the circumstances and your natural way of expressing yourself, you might choose a different word or way of asking this question.

Say you're a financial advisor and a new client comes to you with a $600,000 inheritance. He may not know what to do with it. Under those circumstances, it would make more sense to ask something like, "What do you want to have your money do for you?"

The purpose of this question is to give your client or prospect the opportunity to clearly articulate a future state she or he desires. We like to include the word *whatsoever*—or another word or phrase that reminds people to open the door to what they *really* yearn for, instead of remaining in the anteroom of limited desires.

The following is an example to help make this first question more clear.

> CLIENTS FOREVER: Jim, if you could develop yourself in any area whatsoever, what area would you pick?
>
> JIM: Is this business or life in general?
>
> CLIENTS FOREVER: Well, let's start with business. We could do anything, but let's talk about your business.
>
> JIM: I would develop—try to get rid of my fear of getting larger clients.
>
> CLIENTS FOREVER: Okay. When you say getting larger clients, what are we talking about?
>
> JIM: I'd like to move into, you know, million-dollar clients, a higher level of clientele.

You might have to ask clarifying questions about vague terms so that your client or prospect understands exactly what he or she means. Words like *larger, more, less*, and *smaller* offer a much less specific picture than do phrases like *million-dol-*

lar clients, twice as much business by referral, 20 percent less time, $10,000 less in taxes. The degree to which you help your client get clear about what he or she really wants will determine the power of the revelation he or she experiences.

In the example, Jim was easy. It took only one clarifying question for him to understand and express the fact that he wanted more million-dollar clients. Many people need more than one question. You'll know you've reached the endpoint of asking this question when you hear a clear and measurable (remember Imogene?) answer.

Here's an example of asking multiple clarifying questions:

> CLIENTS FOREVER: If you could develop yourself in any area whatsoever, what area would you choose?
>
> ANDREW: Hmmm. I guess I'd like more business.
>
> CLIENTS FOREVER: When you say more business, what do you mean?
>
> ANDREW: Well, I'm barely making ends meet right now, so I'd like more business.
>
> CLIENTS FOREVER: OK, you'd like so much business that you weren't just making ends meet. How much more business would that be for you?
>
> ANDREW: Gee, I don't really know.
>
> CLIENTS FOREVER: Well, how much is your current level of business generating for you, in terms of income?
>
> ANDREW: About $40,000 a year.
>
> CLIENTS FOREVER: How much income do you think you'd need to have in order to not just be making ends meet?
>
> ANDREW: I guess about $100,000 a year.
>
> CLIENTS FOREVER: So, if you made $100,000 a year, you'd be beyond the point of just making ends meet?
>
> ANDREW: Yes.
>
> CLIENTS FOREVER: Does it matter if you generate that income through more business? Or would you be happy if you could

have that income level doing the same amount of business you're doing now?

ANDREW: I guess it doesn't matter whether I do more business or not. I'd like to make more money.

CLIENTS FOREVER: $100,000 a year?

ANDREW: Yes. That's a good number to shoot for.

In this example, Andrew needed to clarify his goal. He thought he wanted more business, but he really wanted to make more money. By virtue of answering one question, he now knows what he's after.

NEXT QUESTIONS, PLEASE

Once your client or prospect has a clear idea of a circumstance he or she would like to move toward, you can move on. The second question you'll ask is this:

How do you know that _____ is something you need to develop?

As you ask this question, insert into the blank whatever phrase resulted from the last question. Here, again, is Jim's answer:

CLIENTS FOREVER: How do you know that overcoming your fear of having million-dollar clients is something you need to develop?

JIM: Because I don't have those clients now. So, I must have a reason why I don't have those clients.

And here is Andrew's:

CLIENTS FOREVER: How do you know that having an income of $100,000 a year is something you need to develop?

ANDREW: I'm tired of worrying about whether I can pay the bills.

This question helps your client or prospect make an important connection. To answer it, he must make a conscious link between his desire to experience something different and the aspect of his present circumstances that is nudging—or propelling—him in that direction.

No one can motivate someone else. You can persuade or induce them to act in certain ways, but that's quite different than motivating them. Motivation is an internal state. This question—and the next two—give your client or prospect the opportunity to look at the motivation behind his desire to do things differently.

Notice that it doesn't matter whether you agree with the logic behind his answer. Certainly, when Andrew's income increases to $100,000, he could still have trouble paying his bills. Maybe his bills would be proportionately larger, or maybe Andrew has a problem sticking to a budget. But, because you know about the importance of validation, you listen without judging or even commenting on the information your client or prospect shares with you. Your role isn't to probe to find out what the "real" problem might be. You're there to help your client or prospect understand as much as he possibly can about the future he'd like to experience—and what might be motivating him to move in that direction. Andrew wants to pay bills without worrying.

As we said, the next question has a similar purpose. It goes something like this:

When was the last time _____?

What goes in the blank this time is whatever phrase fits, based on the preceding questions.

Here's how the conversations proceeded. Jim is first:

CLIENTS FOREVER: How do you know that overcoming your fear of having million-dollar clients is something you need to develop?

JIM: Because I don't have those clients now. So, I must have a reason why I don't have those clients.

CLIENTS FOREVER: Okay. Jim, when was the last time that you had an opportunity to talk to a bigger client but you backed off or didn't do it?

JIM: Oh—

CLIENTS FOREVER: You thought about calling somebody, thought about talking to somebody and you just didn't?

JIM: I really haven't had an opportunity actually because I'm in a referral level. I need to figure out how to get to that level.

CLIENTS FOREVER: So, let me ask you this. I'm going back to the same question again. How do you know that you need to jump up?

JIM: How do I know I need to?

CLIENTS FOREVER: Uh-huh.

JIM: Oh—

CLIENTS FOREVER: Well, something must not be not working quite the way you want it to or you wouldn't have to go to a higher level of clientele.

JIM: Well, I'm tired of wasting my time on certain types of clients.

CLIENTS FOREVER: Got it.

JIM: The ones I'm trying to train and teach and then they just leave anyway.

CLIENTS FOREVER: Okay. So when was the last time you were involved with some client that you knew was a waste of your time—

JIM: Yesterday.

Andrew's up next:

CLIENTS FOREVER: So when was the last time you felt like that, worried that you couldn't pay your bills?

ANDREW: Last night. No, the night before last.

In Jim's case, this question helped him clarify the experience that was motivating him to seek a change. He wasn't *afraid* of having million-dollar clients; he thought that was the most logical explanation for why he didn't have them. Remember that his answer to the second question wasn't about an experience he'd had. When asked, "How do you know that having million-dollar clients is something you need to develop?" he responded: "Because I don't have those clients now. There must be a reason I don't have those clients." He was expressing feeling puzzled, not fearful.

It was only when Jim started talking about being tired of wasting his time that he dropped down into what's been going on that tells him he needs to change something. That's the *real* reason he wants to change his level of clientele—he's tired and frustrated. Something in your client or prospect's life is telling him to make a change. He becomes aware of it through a personal experience—one with an emotional aspect. The emotions involved can be negative or positive—your client or prospect can be moving away from something he doesn't want to experience or toward something he's already experienced that he wants more of.

When you ask the third question, "When was the last time you experienced that?" the answer is often within the last few days. However, it can be three—or ten—years ago. The reference circumstance is something that has an active place in your client or prospect's conscious mind. More distant experiences are almost always active because they're incomplete. Your clients or prospects don't know how to resolve the incomplete, so they carry it along. They look for something more/better/bigger/different than the experience of the same old load of unfinished business.

Now that you've asked your client or prospect to identify what's really impelling him toward a change, allow him the chance to fully understand the importance of that event or circumstance and how it impacts his life. The fourth question follows naturally:

What happened?

Recalling a particular situation allows your client or prospect to fully access the emotions signaling his desire for change. He basically relives the experience by telling you what it was all about. Your goal is to help him understand, in both logical and emotional ways, what's motivating him to make a change.

As you listen to the response to this question, focus far less on the content of the retelling than on the experience your client is having as he does so. You can see the emotional experience in his face and body language. The angst that Jim felt when his client went against his suggestion, pulled the money out of her IRA, and dumped it into a condo, as you'll read below, was mirrored on his face. The sense of failure that Andrew felt when he couldn't pay the bills came through loud and clear in his slumped shoulders and averted eyes. Their words complete the picture:

> JIM: I've been helping one client for about five years and she wanted to take all of her money out of her IRA to buy a condo. Even though I explained why that made no sense at all, she turned around five minutes later, called my office, and did it anyway.
>
> CLIENTS FOREVER: Uh-huh.
>
> JIM: I'd gone out there recently to do a review and it was a complete waste of my time. She lifted all of her money out anyway.
>
> CLIENTS FOREVER: Yeah. So when you found out that she had taken the money out, how'd you feel?
>
> JIM: Well, you know, I actually felt a bit betrayed that she wasted my time and then did exactly what I told her not to do.

Now it's Andrew's turn:

> ANDREW: I was paying bills the other night, and I had to put off making a payment on my equipment loan so I could pay my assistant. I really hate that.
>
> CLIENTS FOREVER: Yeah.

ANDREW: It's a pain at the time, and I also hate knowing how much the bill will be the next month because I didn't make a payment.

Notice that we asked Jim an additional question. Because his initial answer didn't include a description of how he felt about the situation, we asked him for one. Andrew, on the other hand, spontaneously told us how he felt.

The purpose of the second, third, and fourth questions is to help your client or prospect understand as much as possible about a motivating circumstance. An old saying goes something like, *How can I know what I think until I hear what I say?* The process of speaking tends to help all of us gain more clarity about our experiences. That's why we asked Jim to talk about his. It's possible, even highly likely, that this conversation was the first time he made a conscious connection between a client disregarding his advice and feeling betrayed.

MOVING ON

With the first four questions, you've already helped your client reveal something new to himself—a circumstance in which he's not getting optimal results and how he feels in that circumstance. The ball of revelational buying is gently rolling.

If you were still using a sales technique from another generation, you might do one of two things at this point. First, you could continue to ask your client questions about the circumstance he finds unpleasant; your intention would be to heighten his discomfort so that you could then relieve it by offering a product or service.

We won't mince words. If you're even considering engaging in this kind of blatant manipulation, you've missed the entire point of *Clients Forever*. We know you didn't do the exercises, and you are busted. Put the book down. Put your hands up. Step away from the book.

We'll release you on your own recognizance on one condition—never ever tell anyone that you know anything about seventh-generation sales.

You don't.

The other thing you might do at this point, if you were still following an earlier sales paradigm, is to launch into a presentation. You have a product or service that you think would keep your client or prospect from experiencing the situation he finds unpleasant. You tell him all about it.

Guess what? You've just engaged in gratuitous intimacy. You've asked your client to reveal something very personal—and perhaps painful—to you and now you're using that information for your own purposes. Even if your intention is to help your client, you've abused your relationship.

It's unlikely that your client will say anything to you, largely because you've just destroyed the trust you were starting to create. So we'll tell you how he feels at this point. Like a fool. He was duped into revealing something that was then used against him. Will you get the sale? Your guess is as good as ours. Will you have an extraordinary client relationship? Not a chance.

Incorporating any other sales paradigm into the revelational buying experience does not work. You must either commit fully to the seventh-generation paradigm or stick with what you've been doing up until now. We hope, of course, that you find the seventh-generation approach so refreshing and empowering that you can no longer imagine reverting to a pitch, pitch, pitch way of doing business. Consultative selling has also lost its appeal.

However, it's completely your choice. All we ask is that, if you do decide to use a fifth- or sixth-generation approach, you never use any of the questions we're suggesting here. As we said, that type of usage constitutes gratuitous intimacy. You would be asking your clients and prospects to reveal parts of themselves that they ordinarily wouldn't—and then using that knowledge for your own self-interested purposes. We absolutely can't condone that.

So it's all or nothing, baby. Us or them. Make a choice.

STICKING WITH US?

Good.

Let's move on.

The next two questions you pose allow your client or prospect to understand the long-term implications of the choices he could make.

Question number 5 (actually a closely related series of questions) goes like this:

> *Let's say that situations like these, where you
> _____, continue. Project yourself five years
> down the road. What's that like?*

> *How about twenty years down the road. If you can't
> change this situation, what's that like?*

What goes in the blank in this question is a phrase that captures the motivating circumstance your client or prospect described. Here's how the two conversations we've been following proceeded.

With Jim:

> CLIENTS FOREVER: So let's say that situations like this, where you feel betrayed and like you're wasting time with clients, continue.
>
> JIM: Um-hmm.
>
> CLIENTS FOREVER: Project yourself down the road in another five years. What's that like?
>
> JIM: I'm the person for—for everyone. I'll still work with anyone because I need the business.
>
> CLIENTS FOREVER: How old are you now?
>
> JIM: Thirty-three.
>
> CLIENTS FOREVER: So project down the road about another twenty years and you're fifty-three.
>
> JIM: Um-hmm.

CLIENTS FOREVER: If you can't change this kind of situation, what happens to your career?

JIM: Well, I wouldn't be in this career at fifty-three.

CLIENTS FOREVER: What happens to your self-esteem?

JIM: I wouldn't have any.

And with Andrew:

CLIENTS FOREVER: Let's say that situations like this, where you feel like you don't have enough money to pay your bills, continue.

ANDREW: OK.

CLIENTS FOREVER: Project five years down the line. Where are you? What's that like?

ANDREW: Oh, man. I don't know if I'd even be in this business anymore. I don't think I could stand it.

CLIENTS FOREVER: Now try projecting twenty years down the line. You're how old?

ANDREW: Thirty-eight.

CLIENTS FOREVER: OK, you're fifty-eight and still having trouble paying the bills. Been having trouble doing it for twenty years. What's that like?

ANDREW: I'd have another job, working for someone else. If I'd been crazy and kept doing this, I think I'd be really bitter.

CLIENTS FOREVER: OK.

You've just asked your client or prospect to envision one version of his future. This part isn't fun for your client, so don't linger here. Move on to the next question.

Now let's say that you find a way to turn this situation around, that you're able to _____. What's that like in five years?

What's it like in twenty years?

You probably know by now that what goes in the blank is a phrase that captures whatever your client now understands as the future state he desires. In the first question, you asked in what area your client would develop himself. You can use that information in this question or, if your client's understanding of what he really wants has evolved while you've talked, make sure to include all aspects of your client's desired future state in this question. You're offering him the chance to think big here, so prompt him with all the dimensions that have come up.

Jim responded as follows:

> CLIENTS FOREVER: So, let's say you turn the situation around and find a way to, number one, deal with these types of clients more effectively. More importantly, though, you move to whatever level of client you need to. What would that do for you?
>
> JIM: Well, I would be happier. I'd be more satisfied. I'd have more clients and more money and everything would be wonderful.
>
> CLIENTS FOREVER: Project yourself down the road another twenty years. What's there for you?
>
> JIM: Well, I would be working one day a week and spending the rest of my time with my family and doing my hobbies.

Andrew's response:

> CLIENTS FOREVER: Let's say that you turn your current situation around and you find a way to increase your income to the level you want. We're saying $100,000 right now. What's that like for you?
>
> ANDREW: Well, I don't sweat the bills and I take really nice vacations. I feel proud of how I've built my business, like I'm a success.
>
> CLIENTS FOREVER: Now take that scenario another twenty years down the line. You're fifty-eight, and you've been able to have the income level that you wanted. What's that like?

ANDREW: Huh. I guess I do pretty much what I want to. If I want to work, I do, but maybe I spend a lot of time traveling and doing things that I really enjoy.

CLIENTS FOREVER: Right.

By asking this question, you invite your client or prospect to envision another future. At this point, he has two alternatives in mind. One is unattractive to him—it's the natural unfolding, over time, of the very circumstance that plagues him now. The other future he just envisioned offers him a way out. All he has to do is choose which one to aim for.

By the way, these two questions should seem familiar to you. We posed them to you at the close of the first chapter. Flip back through the pages and take a look at your answers there. Now consider how they influenced your decision to continue reading *Clients Forever*. If you're like many people, the intellectual and emotional process of creating alternate futures increased your motivation to act in a way that moved you toward the future you wanted. In all likelihood, your sense of purpose about transforming your business became more crystallized. You had a clearer idea of what you really wanted.

Notice that what you decided to do after answering those questions didn't depend in any way on *our* understanding your alternate futures. We're not psychic, after all—whatever you wrote down was between you and the page. All we had to do was ask the right questions.

GETTING A MORE SOLID PICTURE OF THE FUTURE

Once your client or prospect has answered the preceding question, they've started building a desirable future. Give them the opportunity to explore what that means to them with a series of two or three follow-up questions.

What would that mean?
What's important about that?

What would that do for you?
What would you know about yourself?

These questions—or similar ones that feel more natural to you—fertilize your client's vision of what he's moving toward. They also balance your conversation. Questions 2, 3, and 4—and the first part of question number 5—ask your client or prospect to recall and reexperience quite a bit of detail about the situation that's motivating him to seek a change. These questions give him the chance to develop just as much detail about the situation he'd like to move toward.

Here are our boys again. This time they get to talk about why they want what they do. First Jim:

> CLIENTS FOREVER: So, let's say you turn the situation around and find a way to, number one, deal with these types of clients more effectively. More importantly, though, you move to whatever level of client you need to. What would that do for you?
>
> JIM: Well, I would be happier. I'd be more satisfied. I'd have more clients and more money and everything would be wonderful.
>
> CLIENTS FOREVER: Project yourself down the road another twenty years. What's there for you?
>
> JIM: Well, I would be working one day a week and spending the rest of my time with my family and doing my hobbies.
>
> CLIENTS FOREVER: What would that mean to you?
>
> JIM: I'd know that I'd been successful.
>
> CLIENTS FOREVER: Why's that important to you?
>
> JIM: Honestly? It sounds kind of corny.
>
> CLIENTS FOREVER: Um-hmm.
>
> JIM: I'd know that I'd made the right choices along the way. I think if you make the right choices, things work for you. And—I wouldn't wonder if I'd been in the wrong place at the wrong time.

CLIENTS FOREVER: Right.

JIM: Yeah.

CLIENTS FOREVER: What message would you be sending?

JIM: To who? The people around me?

CLIENTS FOREVER: OK.

JIM: That I'd had a good life. That everything was good.

And Andrew's response:

CLIENTS FOREVER: Let's say that you turn your current situation around and you find a way to increase your income to the level you want. We're saying $100,000 right now. What's that like for you?

ANDREW: Well, I don't sweat the bills and I take really nice vacations. I feel proud of how I've built my business, like I'm a success.

CLIENTS FOREVER: Now take that scenario another twenty years down the line. You're fifty-eight, and you've been able to have the income level that you wanted. What's that like?

ANDREW: Huh. I guess I do pretty much what I want to. If I want to work, I do, but maybe I spend a lot of time traveling and doing things that I really enjoy.

CLIENTS FOREVER: Right. Why's that important to you?

ANDREW: Life isn't just about struggling. Maybe we all have challenges, but life is about good things, too.

CLIENTS FOREVER: Being able to do those things—work if you want to, do things you enjoy, travel—what would that mean to you?

ANDREW: That I hadn't held back, that I'd gone for it, you know, what I really wanted to do.

CLIENTS FOREVER: Uh-huh. And what would you know about yourself?

ANDREW: I'd know I'd had the courage to try. And I wouldn't regret anything. Maybe there'll still be tough times, but I'd know that I'd really tried. I don't want to be lying on my deathbed, thinking, "If only I'd had the courage to—"

CLIENTS FOREVER: Got it.

It doesn't matter what answers your client or prospect gives. What matters is that he or she gets to take this part of the conversation full steam ahead into a future he or she wants.

THE LAST ONE

There's just one final question. It's very simple.

On a scale of 1 to 10, with 10 being you've got to do something about this and 1 being you don't really care, where are you?

No phrases to fill in here. You just ask your client or prospect to quantify his motivation to act in a way that moves him toward his desired future state.

Back to Jim and Andrew:

CLIENTS FOREVER: Let's say there's a scale of 1 to 10. Ten is you've got to do something about this and 1 is you don't really care. Where are you?

JIM: On a scale of 1 to 10?

CLIENTS FOREVER: Yes. Ten is, by golly, you know, I really need to do something about the kind of clients I have and 1 is *Who cares?* Where are you?

JIM: I'm at 10.

And, Andrew, where are you?

CLIENTS FOREVER: OK, so let's say there's a scale of 1 to 10, with 10 being I've got to do something about my income level and 1 being it doesn't really matter. Where are you?

ANDREW: 10½.

Jim and Andrew answered this question the way that most people do; they rated their motivation to make a change as a 10. For clients and prospects, the process of getting clear about what they do and don't want and envisioning alternate futures is extremely motivating. It's also the first part of a revelation that leads to a decision to buy.

Here's the absolutely wonderful part, the part that blows us away every time we think about it. It blows people away when they realize what just happened, too. Your client or prospect becomes extremely motivated to move toward a particular future *and you never mentioned a product or service.*

We didn't leave anything out of the transcripts. Nowhere did we sneak in a mention of the Clients Forever process. The entire conversations were focused on helping Jim and Andrew become more clear about what they did and didn't want in their lives. This is why revelational buying isn't about selling. It's about creating an environment in which your clients and prospects are free to explore their current and potential future experiences.

This is a very powerful experience. It can literally change someone's life. One of the first times we did this, we had a client that hired us to help train some of their people. Out of seventeen salespeople in their office, they gave us numbers 14, 15, and 17.

Number 16 didn't feel like he needed it, but the sales manager asked him to meet with us anyway.

The four salespeople showed up at the conference room where we were supposed to meet. It was a little tense. We had no rapport, and one gentleman *really* didn't want to be there.

We gave them a list of the seventh-generation questions.

Sam was the name of the man who wanted to be doing anything instead of meeting with us. Sam looked at the questions, and threw the paper back across the table to us. He said, "I'm sure you believe in what you're talking about, but I'm going to tell you something. I'm not going to ask my clients hokey questions like *What would you know about yourself?* I sell a $5000 product over the telephone and I'm not going to ask them."

We said, "Sam, that's because you don't understand it. You're taking it out of context. You need to experience it." He didn't say anything.

So we asked, "What do you do?"

"I'm a salesperson."

We asked him how he started in sales. He told us about selling newspapers as a kid and so forth, what his career had been like. We asked, "So if you could develop yourself in any area, what would you choose?"

Without hesitating, he said, "Closing."

"How do you know that closing is something you need to develop?"

His demeanor—posture and tone of voice—started to shift right then. He got a little softer. "Because I'm not closing the way I need to."

"When was the last time this happened?"

"Yesterday."

"What happened?"

Sam said, "I was on the phone with a client—my fourth phone call with this woman. I know she needs to buy, she knows she needs to buy, and she didn't do it. She wanted to think about it for a few days. Again."

We asked, "If you continue this way, what's going to happen?"

He had the answer right away. "I'm out of here. It's going to have a negative impact on my career and my self-esteem."

We said, "Let's say you turn things around and have the results you want. What's that like?"

He talked about making enough money to build modular housing for homeless people. He'd already completed a prototype.

And then we asked him, "Then what would you know about yourself?"

He started crying.

Within about five minutes, he'd gone from no rapport at all

to tears. He took the Clients Forever questions, changed them a little, and started using them. His sales went up 426 percent in ninety days. That wasn't all that hard to do, because he hadn't been a top performer in the first place. During the next quarter, he was number 3 out of twenty-three salespeople. Within six months, he was also gone—building modular homes.

Now, your clients and prospects may not have as dramatic a response to these questions as Sam did. Rest assured that it's still a very powerful experience for them.

If you've followed the steps we've outlined above, you've succeeded in creating an environment that is completely centered on your client's experience. That's a huge accomplishment.

Let's just pause for a moment here and recognize the enormity of the shift you've made. For centuries, salespeople have controlled and manipulated prospects to make a sale. You've just allowed your clients the freedom to consider whether or not making some kind of a change would be of benefit, without having to simultaneously consider how their choice might impact you. Clients *love* this experience. It's the kind of buying process they could only dream of—until now.

BUT NOW WHAT?

So you're sitting there with a client who's now highly motivated to take a step toward the future she desires. What happens next? You won't be surprised when we tell you what not to do: pitch, present, or take control of the conversation.

Instead, keep the conversation just as client-centered as it's been to this point. Doing anything else would feel like an abrupt disconnection to your client—and to you. The most consistent and natural course to take is to allow your client to decide how much information she needs.

Your client or prospect is now highly motivated to take a step toward a desired future state. She's convinced that she needs something; your job is to point her in the right direction.

If you know that you can help, this is the time to say so. If you operated according to the rules from a previous generation of sales, you might launch into a presentation at this point. Of course, now that you know about the importance of tuning into what your client or prospect wants, you simply point out that you *can* help. *I can help you get there. What information would you like from me at this point?*

Remember that what distinguishes the questions in seventh-generation selling from those in preceding paradigms is *why you want to know the answer*. If you want your prospect to discover for herself whether or not you can help her, you're still in the seventh-generation paradigm. If you'll use the information to qualify or disqualify her, you've moved out of it. Probing questions aren't appropriate.

In a revelational buying experience, your cues about what and how much information to provide come from your client. When clients and prospects realize that a valid path to the future they desire is sitting right in front of them, they want nuts and bolts information about how to work with you. They don't, as a rule, require convincing.

READY TO BUY—FROM SOMEONE ELSE

Of course, you may decide that you *can't* help a client or prospect move toward a desired future. Perhaps you offer a product or service that doesn't completely match what she's looking for. Perhaps you lack the experience or qualifications she wants in a service provider.

You find it easy to refer her on to someone else who might be a better match. In fact, since your primary concern is—and always has been—helping this individual move in the direction she really wants to go, you don't even perceive this as a negative outcome. In the last chapter, we'll talk about how making—and getting—referrals is a natural outgrowth of the seventh-generation approach.

As an example of this kind of thinking, consider a potential client of ours. He's a high-end residential building contractor, specializing in period-perfect restoration of historic homes. The quality of his work is exemplary, and it costs 20 percent more than comparable services from another firm.

In the twenty-three years he'd been in business, this gentleman had never had a marketing plan. More than 90 percent of his business came from referrals; the rest came from inquiries prompted by job signs. He called us because his business had slumped a little. Ultimately, he discovered that it didn't make any sense for him to work with us. Business had fallen off because the general economy had, and even we can't impact that. He decided to tighten his belt and wait things out because he discovered that he was already doing so many things right.

Here's just one of the things he did right—and it pertains to the subject at hand. In the process of talking to potential clients, he took the time to lay out a number of options, only some of which included the job going to his firm. He explored the costs and benefits of approaching a project in a variety of ways, keying into what his prospects cared about most. More than anything, even with his business slipping, he wanted people to get exactly what they were after, even if it meant his firm lost the job. He didn't hesitate to refer prospects to other builders when he thought those other builders would be a better match.

As a result, he even got referrals from people he'd never worked with because they had such confidence in his trustworthiness. The "slump" in his business lasted a single fiscal quarter. He's back up to full steam, with job signs prominently displayed in front of many grand old homes.

READY TO BUY—FROM YOU

Of course, if you're the right person with the right product or service at the right time, your client or prospect will, in fact, buy from you. Congratulations—you've experienced the power and impact of the seventh generation of sales.

All that remains is the details: making sure that what you promise gets delivered, following up, checking back to make sure the client is satisfied. Then you can heave a sigh of relief and move on to the next prospect. Right?

Wrong.

In the seventh generation, a sale is just one part of a long-term relationship. In fact, it's the *relationship* that's rewarding over the long haul.

This relationship—like any other long-term tie in your life—requires maintenance. This shouldn't surprise you. Relationships work when you invest time and energy in them.

And, since seventh-generation sales is qualitatively different from the previous six generations, it shouldn't surprise you that we think of relationship maintenance as substantially more than sending newsletters every quarter and preprinted holiday cards once a year.

CHAPTER 13

THE BUSINESS MARRIAGE

The kind of long-term client relationship fostered by a revelational buying experience is not what you might typically think of as a business relationship. It's far more emotionally fulfilling and financially rewarding.

It requires—and you'll be inspired to give it—your attention, just like you give your attention to all the other long-term relationships in your life. At Clients Forever, we believe that most of the same rules apply to all relationships, whether they're with your spouse, family, friends, or clients. That's why the title of this chapter is "The Business Marriage." (Strictly speaking, we should have called it "Business Polygamy," because you'll have multiple business marriages.)

Fortunately, your nonbusiness relationships make it easier for you to understand what's involved in maintaining relationships, seventh-generation style. Unfortunately, most of your previous experience with taking care of client relationships is probably more akin to a romantic comedy than to a business marriage.

Yes, we mean the kind of romantic comedies you'd see in a theater or rent on DVD. Whether we're discussing *Sleepless in Seattle* or *Bringing Up Baby*, romantic comedies share a common endpoint. The credits usually roll just before or after a wedding. Sometimes, we see a flash-forward into a scene of domestic bliss, but that's icing on the cake. We found out all we needed to when he asked and she said, "Yes."

These plots wrap up in a similar way for a good reason. The fun of watching romantic comedies springs from the tension of wondering if and how two people—too dense to realize how right they are for each other—will pair off. Once they do, we're no longer interested in the story; the tension is resolved.

Previous sales generations take the romantic comedy view of client relationships: the interesting part is getting the commitment. Once a prospect has signed on the dotted line, the tension is over, and you're ready to find another costar. In this view, all the work is over when you get the commitment—at least until you have something else to sell.

That's why marketing takes the place of true relationship maintenance in previous sales paradigms; the real point isn't to maintain a relationship, it's to generate another sale. If you add a personal touch, it might come in the form of a post-transaction thank-you note. After that, though, if you're like most sales professionals, you include some kind of bait in your client contacts: notices about new and upcoming products and services, special offers, and the like.

Do you send a newsletter? If so, find a recent copy and take a good look at it. What "news" does it contain? Probably not much. Most newsletters focus on information about products and what they'll do for the client who's reading the newsletter.

Or, more accurately, newsletters are directed at the clients who are *supposed* to be reading them. What do *you* do with the ones you receive? If you're like most people, you don't read them. Maybe you intend to and set them aside on your desk, where they gather dust until you throw them out. Maybe you scan an article headline before you toss a newsletter into the recycle pile. It's unlikely, though, that you read it word for word.

Your clients don't read newsletters, either. It's tempting to think that yours is categorically different than all the others that clutter up your clients' mailboxes. We have, on very rare occasions, run across newsletters that were so well written and entertaining that they made interesting reading material. Mostly, though, newsletters remind your clients to place you in the same mental category as all the other people who send them junk mail.

Confusing marketing and relationship maintenance is a mistake. It's counterproductive to what you've worked so hard to create: a truly remarkable way of doing business, built for you by your clients, that you find emotionally and financially fulfilling.

Seventh-generation relationship maintenance is simple. All you really have to do is to decide whether you'd treat a spouse, family member, or friend the way you're considering treating a client.

Of course, you know us well enough by now to know that we have plenty more to say on the subject. We offer some very general principles and suggestions below. As you experience being in business marriages, you understand that they're not a matter of calculation or planning. They evolve organically—and your intuition is the best guide to nurturing them.

GETTING YOUR MESSAGES STRAIGHT

We pointed out above that, in previous generations, the point of contacting your clients is to generate more business. So ask yourself, would you only get in touch with your spouse or a friend when you wanted something from them?

How would your relationships fare if you communicated the two-pronged message: *How are you doing?* and *What can you do for me?* How about if you gave gifts on the assumption that you'd eventually receive a financial return on your investment? And how would your spouse or friend respond if your messages included an indirect reminder that you wanted something more from them?

We realize that some people do all these—and more—in their personal relationships. We have, upon occasion, had business or personal relationships with them for whole nanoseconds at a time.

Interestingly, when we refer to mixed messages, we mean more than just words. If your true intention is to drum up business, it doesn't matter how much you pretend otherwise. Your intention seeps into your communication in the form of pregnant pauses, word choice, and the like.

Your client may even be the one who gives you an opportunity to let sales seep into the conversation. Let's say that you found out from someone else that a client of yours had surgery unexpectedly. You call to say that you were just thinking about him. "I'm not calling on business," you might say. "I just heard that you've been out ill. How are you doing?"

Your client might reply along the lines of, "Better, thanks." Now, despite your opening words, he may still think you have an ulterior motive for calling. He probably even *expects* to receive mixed messages, based on his past experience with sales professionals. Why else, after all, would you possibly be calling? He might continue, "We need to get together to go over that proposal you sent me, don't we? I'm pretty backed up after being gone, but how's the week after next?"

It's the easiest thing in the world to say, "Good. When would work for you?" If, in fact, your ulterior motive is as your client suspects, that's exactly what you'll reply. You were hoping all

along that your client would open the door to doing business—
and your interest in his welfare was the pretext you used for
making contact.

If, however, you really *are* calling to see how your client is
feeling, you respond differently. You might say something like,
"At some point, we do need to get together, and I'll call you later
to set up an appointment. Right now, I really just want to know
how you're doing."

These two potential responses convey radically different
messages to your client. One says that he's an entry in your database, and the other conveys that he's a human being who matters to you.

Understand that we're not declaring a moratorium on busi-
ness-related conversations. When you or your company have a
product or service to offer that you think would benefit your
client, you'd be doing him a disservice to keep that information
from him. However, we *are* suggesting that you understand that
this information does not help you keep your relationships with
your ideal clients extraordinary or inspire them to find more
people—just like themselves—to refer to you.

CLIENTS FOREVER Wise Dictum Number 11
*Separate personal communication from product
or sales information.*

GETTING PERSONAL

In order to keep personal communication separate from
product or sales information, you have to have something personal to communicate about.

You may be thinking, *I already do. I send holiday cards that don't contain any product or sales information.*

You might even be thinking, *I already do that. I send holiday* and birthday *cards that don't contain any product or sales information.*

Pardon us for not applauding. This is not what we mean by personal. A perfunctory card once or twice a year does not a relationship make. We'll bet you get holiday cards, too. What do you do with them?

Here's what we do. Every December, we put some of the holiday cards we receive in a location where we can see them throughout the season. They come from family and friends, warm our hearts, and help us remember who's important in our lives. We get cards from our mortgage officer and banker, too— but they don't make it onto the mantel. They go directly into the recycling bin.

However, one card from someone for whom we generate income did make it into our display last year. When instantaneously deciding between "friend" and "business interest," we picked friend.

A couple of things made this card different. It wasn't because of the length of our association with the person who sent it. We've been doing business with this person about as long as we've been working with the same mortgage broker and banker.

Unlike our relationships with those other individuals, however, we touch on personal matters with this person. Our conversations generally start with a personal check-in, based on what we know about each other's lives. Over time, we've found out that we have some similar experiences and circumstances. When we've shared a story or two and a few laughs or sighs of sympathy, we move on to business. We also have strictly business conversations and have had strictly personal ones, as well.

Second, this card was addressed and signed by hand and included a brief personal note. In terms of our relationship, we didn't need a holiday card to tell us that we were more than just another name on a database.

In fact, a holiday card *can't* tell any client that he or she is more than entry number 235 on your list. Relationship maintenance is a year-round activity. You won't make up for months of zero personal contact with a gold-foiled card or a gift basket.

How do you get personal? Just keep your ears open and keep being yourself. In the course of talking with clients, you have the opportunity to exchange lots of information about each other: history, family, priorities, leisure activities, interests outside of business, and sources of pleasure and pride, to name just a few.

If you're identifying with a previous generation of sales, you might solicit or use this information about your client to build rapport. Alternatively, you might see it as filler, something you have to get through to get to the real point: whether or not you can snag a sale. If you're not sure that being yourself is consistent with professional behavior, you might feel awkward about sharing aspects of your own life.

In seventh-generation relationship maintenance, this information *is* the important stuff, the fiber that the two of you weave into a relationship that works. You don't have to elicit it from your client or make a point of mentioning something about yourself. It comes out naturally, as in the following story from a Clients Forever seminar:

> I was talking to a client who wanted to meet with me the following week. I had travel plans; my wife's elderly mother had to move, and we were going to help her pack.
>
> For a split second, I thought about telling him that I needed to go out of town on family business. That's the way we're supposed to talk about stuff like that, right?
>
> Instead, I told the truth. I said that my eighty-seven-year-old mother-in-law needed to move and we were going to help her, and that I could meet the week after.
>
> He told me about his mother and how his sister was taking care of her. She actually lived in the same part of the country as my mother-in-law, so we found out that we'd both grown up in the Midwest, too.

That was the end of our conversation. We made an appointment for the week after I got back. Maybe it's just a coincidence that I got the first referral I'd ever gotten from him about a month later. But I know, for sure, that our relationship is slightly different now; we don't just talk business. We talk about family and vacations and other parts of our lives.

You have travel plans, and one of your clients frequently visits a city that's on your itinerary. Doesn't it make sense to call and ask where to stay and what to see? Let's say that the star pitcher on the high school team is the son of a client, and he's the subject of an article in the local paper. If you were the parent, wouldn't you appreciate a phone call or a note of congratulations?

Notice that we're not talking about elaborate or expensive gestures. We're describing very simple actions that communicate that you notice and value what goes on in your client's life and that you care enough to share what goes on in yours. Successful marriages—business and otherwise—are built on innumerable small gestures of kindness, respect, and consideration.

EXPRESS YOURSELF

You might communicate with your clients in a variety of written forms. Bulk mail, for instance, is the most efficient way to let your clients and prospects know about special offers or product news. As we noted earlier, though, bulk mail rarely helps—and can certainly undermine—your client relationships. Your client's primary response, upon receiving these pieces, is something along the lines of, *Get me out of your database!*

Client-specific standard communications include things like invoices, proposals, and billing and account statements. These items generally have a neutral impact on your client relationships, unless they're full of errors, erasures, and coffee stains.

You might send a business letter for a variety of reasons: to thank clients for their business or support, to solicit donations for a nonprofit organization you're involved with, to answer a question, as a cover letter with a piece of product information, and so forth. Personalizing these communications makes them more meaningful, but don't construe them as being personal communications.

So what's left?

You could send the rarely written—and, consequently, rarely received—letter of appreciation. As far as we know, everyone likes to hear that they're valued and respected—not for how much income they generate for you, but for what they mean to your life.

In fact, despite our best intentions, we don't express our appreciation often enough. We doubt that anyone lying on his deathbed ever thought, "If I'd only told fewer people—and less frequently—how much they meant to me."

Have you ever received a letter of appreciation from someone you respect? We don't mean just a signed thank-you card, but a note or a letter that conveyed something meaningful to you. In most Clients Forever workshops, we ask participants that question. Invariably, nearly everyone has; it's also noteworthy that most people have only received a few, no matter how long they've been in business.

We then ask what happened to the letter or note, and nearly everyone indicates that they kept it. *How long?* we ask. In a recent workshop, the answers ranged from seven to forty years. A year or so back, one Clients Forever workshop participant told us about keeping a thank-you letter for forty-three years.

This is clearly the opposite of a preprinted holiday card.

People don't keep letters thanking them for spending money, the "I appreciate your business" kind of note that we commonly send and receive. People do keep letters that refer to specific actions or qualities you appreciate or that tell them how they've impacted your life.

Here are some phrases from letters of appreciation we've received that convey the spirit of what we mean:

Thank you for your commitment to helping people.

You have a wonderful ability to get right to the heart of the matter.

Thank you for your art and your care.

I just want you to know how much I appreciate your candor and directness.

The impact of working with you will stay with me for a very long time.

A few characteristics distinguish letters of appreciation from all other kinds of business communication. They're entirely personal and all about the person to whom they're written. Letters of appreciation get much more mental play than they do page life—we tend to think about sending them and fail to follow through.

Nearly everyone recognizes the importance and impact of letters of appreciation; why don't people write more of them? Clients Forever clients and participants often name a couple of reasons, right off the bat. They don't have enough time. They get caught up doing other things. Despite what they say, though, we believe that one reason people don't send more letters of appreciation is that they don't know what to say.

Letters expressing your appreciation are natural responses to people who've had a significant impact on your life. Often, strong feelings—of gratitude or respect—inspire them. These very feelings can also prevent you from putting pen to paper. You feel inadequate to the task of conveying appreciation for something that you feel so strongly about. You may fear that your words won't get the message across, that you'll botch it up. So, instead of writing a letter, you continue to think about doing it.

Let's look at what it takes to write a letter of appreciation that works. In the space below, list three to five people who've had a significant impact on your life—relatives or friends, teachers or mentors, people who were there for you when you least expected it.

If your experience is typical of most Clients Forever clients and workshop participants, you've already expressed your appreciation to one or more of these people. If their name comes up again here, it's because their impact on your life was very significant. Now consider this question: If you could only write a letter of appreciation to one person on the above list, who would it be?

Circle that person's name.

Now find something to write with and a sheet of blank paper. *Any* sheet. One reason people avoid writing a letter of appreciation is that they have to find a sheet of paper that's worthy of the message they intend to convey: a handmade piece of parchment or Italian silk rag paper, say. Bull-pucky.

Use your letterhead or grab a piece of paper out of your printer. If *that's* too hard, borrow a sheet of wide-ruled school paper from your son or daughter. At this point, we'll brook no excuses having to do with a lack of writing materials, so get something to write on and something to write with. If you're sitting on a remote beach or on an airplane, rip a largely blank page out of this book. *Do not* read on until you have it. We mean it.

Now that you have paper in hand, check out whether the size feels right to you. Feeling intimidated by too much blank space can also keep you from writing a letter of appreciation. Tear your piece of paper in half if you want to. Or go back to your desk and get an index card. One of the first letters of appreciation we ever wrote was on a three-by-five index card, and, despite its humble appearance, the recipient was deeply touched.

If you're hesitating because you don't have an address for the person to whom you want to express your appreciation, get your pen or pencil moving, anyway. The hard part isn't finding out where to send a letter; the hard part is getting your thoughts down on paper. If it's important for you to send the letter, you'll find the address.

You have the materials at hand, so start. Tell the truth. If you don't know how to begin, then you can use these words: *I've been sitting here thinking about you, and I appreciate you for* . . . Beyond the introduction, we're not going to give you much of an example because, in our experience, you may be tempted to use our wording instead of your own. So you fill in the blank: something the recipient did or said, their characteristics, traits, or qualities that touched you and made a difference in your life. Your fifth-grade teacher's enthusiasm and care. Your mother's patience and faith. Your sister's support. There's no right or wrong about what's important to you, so don't second-guess your impulses here.

Don't erase. Don't edit. Just keep going. The person who reads your letter won't care if it's typewritten or scrawled, grammatically perfect or misspelled. The crucial element is your desire to convey how important this person has been in your life.

You have to trust that what you want to say is exactly what the recipient wants to hear: that no one could come up with a more meaningful or on-target expression of gratitude than you can.

The more specific you can be, the better. What did someone say that made a difference in your ability to believe in yourself? How did someone support you when you least expected it? When did you feel a sense of connection that gave you an unanticipated lift?

Stop when you've run out of things to say. If you're done after two sentences, good for you. You win the Clients Forever brevity prize. If you want to continue onto another page, go ahead. You can be sure that the person who's reading your letter won't stop because it's too long; after all, it's about a favorite subject—him- or herself.

Sometimes, people hesitate to send a letter of appreciation because they're unduly concerned about how the recipient will respond. He might feel obligated to acknowledge the letter or reciprocate. She might feel like it's a little too personal. He might doubt your motives.

In our experience, people who receive letters of appreciation uniformly love the experience. If you truly don't want the recipient to feel he or she should respond, you'll convey that. You're expressing what you felt and experienced, so it's highly unlikely that you'll offend someone or invade that person's personal boundaries. And you're keeping the message clean by not mixing *thank you* with *can I have more?*, so your recipient trusts that your intention is what you say it is—to convey gratitude.

IT REALLY IS THE THOUGHT THAT COUNTS

One of the many things we do in Clients Forever workshops is ask participants to rank various ways they could potentially receive a message of appreciation. Two methods always come out as numbers 1 and 2. A handwritten letter is the most powerful way to express your gratitude to someone else; the effort that you put into creating the message and the form is obvious.

Number 2 is a handwritten card that appears personally selected, the kind of item you'd find at a bookstore or gift shop. A personally selected card speaks volumes about the effort behind finding a card that matches your sentiment and the recipient.

Notice that neither of these—more meaningful than most gifts or flowers—costs more than a couple of dollars. So the value of your appreciative gesture corresponds more to the thought you put into it than the cash you spend on it.

For instance, sending a gift basket doesn't take much thought on your part; all that's required is a phone call and a charge card. Ditto for standard floral arrangements. However, adding a personal note or hand-delivering either one of these increases their perceived value.

You can even outspend your recipient's comfort level. We once received a very expensive gift that was out of scale to our relationship with the sender. A very short note accompanied it. A better option for expressing gratitude would have been a longer note and a less ostentatious gift.

WHAT'S ENOUGH?

How do you make sure you contact your clients—with personal phone calls, letters, and notes of appreciation—in a way that fosters extraordinary relationships?

Sheer persistence certainly isn't the answer. A few years ago, we bought an expensive sports utility vehicle. The salesperson called the next week to thank us for the purchase, see how the vehicle was performing, and ask if we had any questions. We were pleased with the follow up.

A couple of weeks later, he called to thank us again and make sure we knew the right number to call for an appointment when the first service was due. We were surprised at the thorough follow up and pleased at how thoughtful he was.

He called again a couple of weeks after *that*. We can't recall what the reason for the third phone call was—other than to thank us one more time—but he left a message that we didn't return. We were no longer pleased; we suspected he'd never made another sale. We imagined him sitting by the phone in a barren showroom cubicle, counting the days until two weeks had gone by and he could call us again.

You get the point. The right amount of contact is a terrific thing. Too much contact is just plain weird.

But, you might be wondering, *what's the right amount of contact?* What combination of timing and gestures says, *You're far more than just a name in my database*, but stays well out of *I have no life* territory?

Trust yourself. Reconnect with the feelings you have when you're in relationship with an ideal client (you listed them in Chapter 10) and trust your gut. If you're thinking about a particular client, give that person a call. If an article in a publication reminds you of a conversation you recently had with a prospect, copy it and send it off. If you're thinking of someone you haven't spoken to in a long time, it's because you need to contact her.

There are no hard and fast rules for a happy Clients Forever business marriage. We know of, however, one basic rule and two approaches to writing letters and notes of appreciation.

Here's the rule. You have to do it. That's easy enough to say, right? It's even easy to commit to doing—at least once or twice. But we'll bet there are about a gazillion other things to fill your week.

Pick your rocks. Steven R. Covey tells a story in the book *First Things First* that might be familiar to you. A teacher puts a jar on a table in front of his class. He fills it with big rocks and asks the class if the jar is full. The class agrees that it is. The teacher then pours gravel in the jar and asks again if it is full. The class members are less certain. The teacher pours sand into the jar, filling the small spaces between the pieces of gravel, and finally adds water, filling it to the top. The point the teacher was making was not how much a jar can hold, but that filling it to the brim required that the rocks, gravel, sand, and water go in in a certain order. Most importantly, the rocks have to go in first.

The rocks are the items on your agenda that are important, but not urgent. They form the foundation of your personal and business life, yet you easily overlook them in favor of more urgent, but less important, concerns. In other words, you forget about rocks when you have sand in your shorts.

But, in the seventh generation, the rocks are more than the right thing to do. You'll *want* to put the rocks in first when you experience the fulfillment and power of an extraordinary relationship with an ideal client. You still have to figure out exactly how to do so, and this is where the two approaches we mentioned earlier come in. Either method—or a combination of the two—can work for you.

First, there's the freeform approach to appreciating your clients. You write cards and letters whenever you have time. If you travel, for instance, writing notes of gratitude is a good way to spend plane or hotel room time. All you need to do is carry inventory (cards, writing paper, writing utensil, stamps) and addresses.

Approach B is the scheduled approach. You create a small block of time each week to write one letter of appreciation. Every Thursday afternoon at three o'clock, for example, you schedule a thirty-minute thank-you session. Either method works; just choose the style that fits you best.

A related issue is when—and how often—to extend your appreciation to a specific person. Again, the answer is: Whenever it strikes you. If that person is the one who comes to mind when you sit down with paper and pen, go for it. According to this nonplanned plan, one individual might get a note from you four times in five months.

Someone else might hear from you three times a year—in April, November, and January, for instance. Or May, July, and February. The months and interval don't matter. As your relationship develops, your points of contact and gestures of appreciation don't require a lot of thought. Either one of you picks up the phone when you need to and you both know that the role you play in each other's life is valuable.

However, the very irregularity of your gestures is striking; your extraordinary clients can't help but pay attention to how important to you they are. (Their predictable arrival, by the way, is why occasion cards [warning: *Clients Forever* technical term ahead] suck. Cards that have nothing to do with holidays, birthdays, anniversaries, or any of the occasions created by the greeting card industry say, *Dang, you really* were *thinking about me.*)

THE RISK OF BEING BUSY

You already know why you want to send the message to your clients that they're important to you. Relationship maintenance, seventh-generation style, keeps your extraordinary client relationships healthy. It's all part of the seventh-generation package that leads to a life you love, built for you by clients who love you.

Being busy working with extraordinary clients is a terrific thing. It's exactly what you were hoping to create. But it has a potential downside.

Looking or *sounding* busy can undermine what you've created. This is a simple concept. Think how your spouse or friends would feel if you constantly projected an *I'm so busy* message. All your relationships would deteriorate.

In addition, if you send out busy signals, your clients may also question your ability to follow through on what you said you'd do. They may wonder if your busy-ness means that you don't have the time you need to do a great job. And, in the next chapter, we'll talk about how looking and sounding busy impacts your clients' willingness to refer other people to you.

Here are some things you might inadvertently or unconsciously do that send a busy signal to your clients and prospects. You may speak rapidly or fail to enunciate your words adequately. You might sigh as you sink into a chair or in the middle of a conversation; certainly, repeatedly checking the time on your wristwatch communicates the message that you don't have much to spare. Perhaps you comment that you only have a few moments for a conversation or make or take calls in the middle of a meeting.

Maybe you mention that you come to work early, go home late, take work home with you, work on the weekends or on holidays, or would like to have more time for yourself or your family. Other busy signals include passing clients' questions or routine matters to someone else, delaying completion on tasks or jobs for days or weeks, and leaving someone on hold for more than a few seconds.

It's probably clear that these often unconscious behaviors will work against your goal of communicating to your clients that they're important to you. So, with business booming, how do you send the message that you have plenty of time?

The ideas that follow won't solve all of the time management challenges you may face, but they'll give you some practical ideas you can put into use immediately.

Create a Ritual

Anyone can look good when things are going smoothly—when your car and all your meetings start on time, when you go directly from point A to point B without unplanned detours to points F, P, and W. When your day—or week—falls apart, though, you need a first line of defense against frantic busy signals.

When Murphy's law is operating in overdrive, do what great athletes do. When you watch a tennis match between top-seeded players, you may notice them examining or adjusting the strings of their tennis rackets between points. The strings don't need to be adjusted, but the best tennis players in the world have trained themselves to perform a ritual between points. It helps them maintain their concentration no matter what's happening in the match.

Baseball pitchers and batters, track and field athletes, basketball players facing a free throw—they all use rituals to pace themselves and gain emotional control and mental focus. So create a ritual for yourself, too.

Just be silent for ten seconds. That's the whole ritual. Before any appointment, simply stop what you're doing and sit or stand silently for a full ten seconds. At the end of ten seconds, take a deep breath and let it out. Then proceed with your appointment.

Slow and Easy Does It

After a ten-second pause, make a deliberate, slow movement. You can choose to do something as simple as standing up and walking over to your client or prospect, making eye contact, and shaking hands. The key is to move slowly and deliberately. Spending two extra seconds will send the message that you consider the person you're greeting important.

Enunciate Vowels

If you're like most people, you tend to emphasize the consonants of your spoken words when you're in a hurry. This makes you sound clipped and unemotional. So, particularly when you're feeling rushed, pay attention to enunciating your vowels.

This effort will create two results. First, you'll express yourself with more passion and compassion; your comments will be more lively. You and your client will both be more emotionally involved in the conversation, leading to a greater likelihood that you'll feel more connected with each other.

The second effect of enunciating your vowels is that your word speed will tend to be slower, which will give your conversation more impact and make it feel more satisfying to both of you.

Move Away from the Desk

Have important conversations at a location other than your regular desk. If someone steps into your office to ask a question, stand up or move around and lean on the front edge of your desk. For formal appointments, move away from your desk and sit with your client at a different location: a table, two armchairs, a conference room.

A Pause That Matters

Even though you may be listening carefully, your conversation may still take on an air of hurriedness. You may respond, for instance, to the other person before she has completed saying what she wanted to say.

We suggest that, before responding, you wait for at least two full seconds after the other person stops speaking. This ensures that he has finished and gives you time to consider your response. A business acquaintance of ours puts his telephone on mute during conference calls so he can concentrate more fully on what the other people are saying. If a question is directed at him, he needs to release the button before he can speak. He says this practice gives him a moment to collect his thoughts before he speaks.

Walk the Walk

When your clients leave your office, escort them to the door or lobby. This simple gesture of respect helps you in a few ways. First, it shows your client or prospect that you're not simply waiting for him to leave so you can get on to the next task. Second, it gives you another opportunity to shake hands and maintain your connection. And finally, you have time to think about your next task or appointment as you walk back to your desk. The change of scenery will help clear your head, and organizing your thoughts will take the same amount of time whether you're seated or on your feet.

Using these suggestions can help you send the strong message to your clients that they belong to a very special group of people for whom you always have time. Your extraordinary clients *are* important to you, and these suggestions help you remember that fact—even when the phone is ringing and your email inbox is overflowing.

In the final chapter of *Clients Forever*, we'll talk about how the same principles reassure your clients and make it easier for them to build your business—and a new kind of community—for you.

CHAPTER 14

A COMMUNITY OF
LIKE-MINDED
INDIVIDUALS

We've been saying all along that one of the results of the seventh-generation approach is a life that you love, built for you by clients you love. We've talked about how to know what's most important to you and how that helps you to be more fully yourself and more present in your relationships with clients and prospects. We've talked about how your real role is to create an environment in which your clients feel free to be fully themselves—to experience a revelation that connects their current experience with their most desired future states.

This is all good stuff, a radical new way of thinking about what sales is—and what it isn't. If you're like most people who go through the Clients Forever process, you've already experienced some of its benefits firsthand.

However, we haven't talked about what any of this has to do with building your business. The truth is that we could get away without talking about it, because, over time, your clients would naturally expand your business for you.

ORNITHOLOGY 101

The following paragraphs explain why.

We're operating on the premise that your clients and prospects are just as smart as you are. (Your choice of reading material reveals your obvious intelligence.) They will figure out, eventually, that the two of you belong to a unique community of like-minded people.

We don't know who first said it, but it's true: Birds of a feather flock together. The community or flock you're both part of includes many individuals. You know some, and your client or prospect knows some; you may even know a few individuals in common—people who express themselves honestly and openly, who know who they really are and what's important about life.

It's natural that, over time, you would introduce each other to people who are part of this like-minded community. Whether for social or business reasons, the two of you naturally extend your connections.

As an aside, let us just point out that people who aren't part of a like-minded community similar to what we describe pay money to extend their connections through networking groups, where the like-mindedness that members share is needing more business. Let's see . . . on the one hand, you could meet people who know who they really are and what's important and express themselves honestly and openly. On the other hand, you could meet people who need more business.

Not only have we changed your life, we've just saved you the annual dues of a networking group. No applause necessary.

Over time, your clients would build your business for you because they'd just naturally want you to meet other people who are like them.

A MORE SYSTEMATIC APPROACH

However, you can also help your clients understand that they're part of a unique community. In the process, you can also get solid referrals to individuals who are precisely the sort of people you want to work with.

In Chapter 10, we asked you to fully flesh out your description of your ideal client. Lo, these many chapters ago, describing your ideal client helped you understand exactly who you want to work with. We're going to return to that concept here, but for a different reason.

Here, we're going to use the notion of ideal clients to help you figure out how to find *more* of them. This, by the way, isn't a new idea. People in financial services, for example, can rattle off numerical descriptions of the kind of clients they really want to work with.

> *They're worth X dollars.*
> *They make X dollars and have Y dollars in assets.*
> *They make X dollars, have Y dollars in assets, and are willing to pay me Z dollars to manage their assets.*

Typically, when sales professionals think about building their businesses, they think about finding more clients who meet these economic conditions. That's all very well and good, but, as we pointed out, nearly everyone has (or had, if they're lucky) a client who met their economic criteria but was an unmitigated PITA (Pain in the Area).

It's not fun to work with PITAs. PITAs don't build your business for you. And you can allow PITAs to turn you into the business equivalent of a prostitute.

We suggest that you make the radical decision that you only want to work with clients who fit, or come very close to fitting, your ideal. No more PITAs. No more partial PITAs. Make that choice for yourself—and read on to find out how to make it a reality.

JETTISON THE PITAS

Start by firing your PITAs as clients. We're serious. The only way you can avoid this step is if you've already done it.

In the first chapter, we told you about Steven McGuffey and Bill Fernandez, who sold off the portfolios of nearly 600 merely ordinary clients. They weren't even releasing PITAs. If you're like most people, you'll jettison a few, rather than a few hundred, clients.

Of course, you probably won't put this book down, go make a few phone calls, and return to the page PITA-free. You'll give some thought to the matter. Will you refer these individuals on or simply release them? What will you tell them by mail or over the phone? You can handle this matter however you'd like, but we'd suggest (no surprises here) that you tell the truth. You've redefined your business and are moving in a new direction; you'll no longer be able to offer your services.

Don't worry about the income your PITAs generate. In our experience, the noneconomic costs of PITAs outweigh their monetary merits; you pay for them in blood, sweat, and tears. Second, when you make space for new clients by releasing PITAs, new clients appear. We won't promise that they'll materialize mere seconds after your final PITA handshake, but the kind of clients you really want to work with will eventually show up. And we'll walk you through a process that will make them appear more rapidly.

In the space below, list the PITAs you're going to fire. *I release. . . .*

from doing business with me by _____.

What goes in the blank is a date, no more than thirty days from the present date, by which you'll release these clients.

DO THE MATH

Now that you've made a commitment to yourself to jettison your PITAs, you can proceed free, at least mentally, from the need to consider them part of your business.

First, some theory. The Pareto principle, also known as the 80/20 rule, holds that 80 percent of your results come from 20 percent of your efforts. In terms of your clients, you could expect that 20 percent of your clients would generate 80 percent of your results.

In our experience, both numbers are off. It's more like a 50/8.6 rule; 50 percent of your results come from 8.6 percent of your clients. In other words, you could increase your business 50 percent with only 8.6 percent more effort.

Clearly, you need to know your own numbers.

On a separate sheet of paper, list your clients in order of the income they generated for you over the last calendar year, from highest to lowest, running a cumulative total as you go along. For instance, let's say your first four clients are Client A, who generated $15,000, Client B, worth $9000, Client C $5000, and Client D $3750.

The first part of your list would look like this:

Client A	$15,000
Client B	$24,000
Client C	$29,000
Client D	$32,750

Go ahead and make your list now. Wait to read on until you've done so. This process hinges on you having some specific information available from your list.

Now draw a line under the client who represents the halfway point of your income; that is, roughly 50 percent of your income came from the clients above this individual and 50 percent came from clients farther down on your list. In the example above, let's say you made $56,000 in the last year. Client C represents the halfway point, because your income passed $28,000 as a result of this individual's business.

Take a look at the names below the line you drew. If you're like most people, they represent the vast majority of your clients—and contribute a disproportionately small amount of results.

Here's why most businesses have a similar distribution of results among their clients. When you start a business, you normally need any business you can get. Your only criterion for taking clients is if they can fog a mirror. As you develop a client base and some confidence, you work into higher and higher value clients—and you keep the original client base, too. They're nice people, and you may have admirable and compelling feelings of loyalty to them.

Our point is, though, that when you expand your business, you want to include more clients like those *above* the line you drew. They're the ones who contribute the most to your financial well-being.

And, because you already weeded out the PITAs who might have been above the line, you know that these are people who you want to work with. Whether or not you further distill your clientele by releasing some of the individuals below the line is up to you, but realize that McGuffey and Fernandez sold the portfolios of clients who fell below a line they drew (at a cutoff point unknown to us) on their client list.

LOOK FOR THE COMMON THREAD

You now have a list of select clients. Which of these are your favorites? Who do you really enjoy working with among the individuals who provide the best results for your business?

Make a list of five or so in the space below. You don't have to consider their economic characteristics any longer because you already narrowed your list down to the top earners.

My favorite clients are. . . .

If there's someone on the other part of your list that you want to include here, do. Keep a heart case. Most of us have people that we continue to work with, sometimes gratis, because we like them so much or see an opportunity to contribute something substantial to someone else's life.

Now ask yourself two questions. First, what do you like about the people whose names you just listed? What are the qualities that earn them entry into your list of favorites?

Here's how one person answered this question:

> They're open-minded, but they're also opinionated and not afraid to express their opinions. They have a sense of humor and can engage in banter with me. They're also serious about getting results; intense in kind of a relaxed way.
>
> Once they get into something they're excited about, they don't let go. Like a puppy with a chew toy, they keep at it until they're satisfied.

Your answers will obviously be different. Take the time to list the things that you really enjoy about each individual. Jot them down in the space below without attributing them to a particular person. Notice that some qualities appear differently in different people. For instance, a sense of humor can be wry or wild and crazy. Some decisive people act quickly; others consider their options carefully. What is it that makes working with these people so enjoyable?

I like these individuals because . . .

Now ask yourself a second question. How do you feel when you're working with these individuals? Again, here's an answer that a Clients Forever participant gave.

> I don't feel like I have to prove anything. I'm trusted and respected and we're doing things together.

In the space below, answer this question for yourself. *When I'm working with my favorite clients, I feel . . .*

DEBUNKING REFERRALS

The next step is to invite these individuals to build a community of like-minded people with you. This constitutes the Clients Forever process of asking for referrals. But first, we must make a necessary side trip so you can understand the differences between what you think asking for referrals is like and what we're suggesting you do.

If you're like most people who are learning about the seventh generation, two things are true about your experience with asking for referrals. First, you know you're supposed to do it. After all, entire systems of business development are predicated on your willingness and ability to extract the names of likely prospects from your current customers, friends and family, casual acquaintances, and near strangers.

Second, if you're typical, you don't ask for referrals, because it's uncomfortable for you to do so. In fact, we're racking our collective brains, trying to remember if we've ever met anyone who truly enjoyed the process. The outcome can make it worthwhile, but, on the whole, asking for referrals is like getting a tooth pulled without Novocaine. It's such a relief when it's over.

We're about to let the cat out of the bag about referrals. There are compelling reasons why you, in all likelihood, either avoid asking for them or think of them as prune juice for your business—something distasteful that keeps everything working.

Let's imagine a typical asking-for-a-referral scenario. Your client purchased a product or service that is well worth what she paid. She's satisfied, you've been compensated; you both received value from your relationship. Neither one of you owes the other anything, and your relationship is in balance.

Now let's say that you like this client; your relationship to this point has been enjoyable—and ordinary. By asking for a referral, you ask for something that you can't repay. This violates a cultural value of reciprocity—*scratch my back and I'll scratch yours*. You're asking for a free backscratch.

Your client can't simply overlook your request, either. You've created an obligation that your client is unable to ignore. Even if she doesn't respond, it remains an incomplete issue for your client, as burdensome as any other incomplete.

Your client may give you a putoff.

I can't think of anyone right now.
Gee, I don't know anyone who'd be a good referral for you.

Perhaps your phone calls stop getting returned because your client wants to avoid being asked for a referral again. Or your client squeezes out the name of someone who turns out to be a low-quality referral. Sound familiar?

Moreover, if you ask your client to refer you to someone in a particular income bracket, you're asking for what is generally held to be confidential information. You're asking your client to break trust with someone else for your benefit.

The end result of asking for a referral in an ordinary relationship is often a damaged relationship. Not long ago, a casual business acquaintance invited us out to join him for a cup of coffee "to catch up." We liked this guy, so we made the time to go. It quickly became apparent that he had recently started a financial planning business with a multilevel marketing enterprise. He didn't want to catch up, he wanted referrals. We didn't owe him anything and felt that he had presumed on our casual friendship. Not only did we fail to give him a referral, we stopped taking his calls.

The bottom line is that we're surprised that asking for referrals from ordinary clients *ever* works. Making your clients uncomfortable, imposing a burden, setting your clients up to avoid you or tell you less than the truth to keep from disappointing you, asking them to violate a relationship with someone else—asking for referrals creates these unhappy dynamics.

It should be clear to you by now that none of these scenarios are consistent with the seventh generation. We've spent a lot of pages helping you build unique, valuable, trusting relationships with your clients and prospects. The very last thing we'd do at this point is recommend a course of action that would undermine or end those relationships.

So, in contrast, consider a more meaningful relationship that you currently have with someone. When and if this individual asked for help, how would you or did you feel? If you're like many people, you felt honored to be of assistance. In the context of a close and trusting relationship, help requested and rendered *strengthens* the relationship.

Balance is also far less of an issue. In any long-term relationship, the pendulum of reciprocity swings more slowly. Even if the other individual owes you a favor or two, you know you'll eventually be repaid.

Asking for a referral from an extraordinary client is an altogether different matter than asking for a referral from anyone else. And, in seventh-generation sales, you're doing far more than simply asking for a referral.

REALIZE WHAT YOU'RE UP TO

First, forget what asking for a referral is supposed to get you: a name with a phone number attached to it. In fact, you don't want to *get* anything.

This is an important—and somewhat subtle—point. In our experience, it's very likely that you will, in fact, receive the names of one or more people with whom you'll really enjoy working. However, if that's your primary motivation for embarking on the process we describe in this chapter, your clients are likely to assume that you're simply asking for a referral. And, since we just described what happens when you ask for a referral, you're probably highly motivated to approach the process from an entirely new perspective.

Here it is: You want to *build* something that will benefit both you and your client. You want to expand and strengthen the community of like-minded people that includes the two of you.

What distinguishes the Clients Forever process from asking for referrals is the fact that it benefits both you and your client. Building a community of like-minded people isn't simply a new way to frame a request for a referral. It addresses a basic human desire.

Feeling part of a community—a web of positive interconnections with others—gives life more meaning and opens the door to richer experiences. It confirms our impact on and importance to the world around us. We doubt very much that anyone in the depths of despair ever thought *If I died tomorrow, too many people would miss me.*

Most of us are already part of a number of intersecting or overlapping groups, defined by geography, religious affiliation, professional, leisure or charitable activities, or any number of other characteristics. The difference between a group and a community is that the latter feels like home.

That's why we refer to it as a community of like-minded people. Maybe the whole community never exists in the same place at the same time. In fact, it probably includes people from around the world. The point is that they are your tribe, the people with whom you feel a core affinity.

You might invite your client to join you in building this community with words like those that follow. Of course, you'll find the ones that work for you. Remember, too, that you don't need to script them in advance—trust yourself to say exactly what you need to.

> Look, one of the things I really enjoy about being with you is that I feel like we're part of the same community. There are people in my life that you need to meet. There are probably people in yours that I need to meet. I believe that we're all part of the same like-minded community, whether or not we ever do business together.
>
> If we're going to build a community that works for all of us, I need your help. Really, just so you know, I'm looking for another you. Who do you know who's open-minded but has opinions and isn't afraid to express them? They have a sense of humor and like to banter. They're also intense in kind of a relaxed way. Most importantly, when you're with them, you feel like you're doing things together and that you're trusted and respected. Who do you know who's just like you?

In this statement, or something like it that comes more naturally to you, you've also given your client two other gifts. First, you've offered an accurate description of how they show up in the world. Without exaggeration, overstatement, or flattery, you've enumerated the things you like about your client. Very few people receive specific feedback about how others perceive them—and all, or at least most, of us would like to.

Second, you've just declared their importance to you—as a *person*, not a source of income. You've acknowledged that you're not two people operating separately, you're two parts of one community that is very important to you.

THEN WHAT?

That's it. You're done. Your client is free to pass along a name or two—or simply receive the feedback and move along. You haven't imposed an obligation. You haven't bruised your relationship—you've bolstered it.

In reality, people pass names along. And they tend to be very high-quality referrals. Because most of us are our own worst critics, your clients see the positive attributes you mention in other people more easily than they see them in themselves. They tend to refer you to people who are like themselves—or even better.

There are two more steps to this process. When your client mentions a name, ask why she or he thought of that particular individual. "What do you like about Joe? What made you think of Joe?" Repeat that information when you contact the referral. For instance:

> Hi, Joe. Sam told me that you were someone he really likes being in relationship with, that you have a great sense of humor, you're intelligent, decisive, and a great problem solver. He always feels respected and trusted and that you approach things as a team.

By repeating your client's reasons for referring you to this particular person, you strengthen the relationship between the *two of them.* In all likelihood, Joe had only a limited awareness of how important their relationship was to Sam. Strengthening their relationship also strengthens the entire community of like-minded people.

By introducing yourself in this way, you also establish the condition of that community. Your words convey the powerful message, *We tell the truth about what we think and feel.*

The other step that we've found beneficial is to ask your client if she would be willing to make an introductory phone call to the referral. In most cases, this favor is no problem. However, if she's not willing to make the call, you shouldn't make it, either.

The most remarkable response to this process that we ever heard of came from a coaching client of ours. He had this conversation with a friend he'd love to—but didn't—have as a client. His friend promptly downloaded the names, phone numbers, and addresses of fourteen people from his Palm Pilot into our client's. On average, people tend to receive about four names each time they have a conversation with a client like the one we just described.

Is this going to hold true for you? Who knows? It'll happen for you the way it's going to. And, if you understand the spirit behind inviting your clients to build a community with you, you'll also understand that it doesn't matter if you get one name or ten—or none.

We do know, though, that many people have found this community-building endeavor to be a remarkably effective way of both enhancing their existing client relationships and expanding their business to work with the kinds of people they really want to. By being open and vulnerable, generous and honest, your life and your business are utterly transformed.

There's an old adage about business that goes like this: It isn't what you do that matters, it's who you know. At Clients Forever, we believe that it isn't who you know that matters, it's who knows you. The real you.

INDEX

About the Authors

Doug Carter, founder and CEO of Carter International Training and Development Company, has been a sales professional and trainer for more than twenty-five years. Since 1988, he's conducted his own training and interactive speaking prorgams. He also develops and delivers custom training programs for organizations throughout the country.

Jenni Green is a freelance commercial writer and marketing consultant.